Ontario's
Old Mills
by
Harold Stiver

Ontario's Old Mills
A Guide for Photographers and Explorers

Copyright 2012 Harold Stiver

ISBN #978-0-9868670-1-9

All rights reserved. No part of this book may be reproduced in any form or by any electronic or mechanical means including information storage and retrieval systems without permission in writing from the author, except by the reviewer who may quote brief passages

Photo Credits
All Photographs are the Copyright of Harold Stiver and cannot be used without his express written consent.

For *my wife Elaine, for everything*

Table of Contents

How to use this Book   Page 7
Photographing Historic Mills   Page 9
Milling in Ontario   Page 11

List of Mills
Western Ontario Region

Brant County   Page 13
Apps Mill, German Woolen Mill Ruins, St. George Mill
Bruce County   Page17
Arranvale Mill, Fisher Grist Mill, McCullough Mill, McClure's Mill, Mildmay Chopping Mill, Parkhead Chopping Mill, Pinkerton Mill, Scone Mill, Stark's Mill (Paisley City Roller Mills)
Grey County   Page 27
Ayton Mill, Ferguson Gristmill, Flesherton Mill, Herb Miller Saw Mill, Holstein Mill, Inglis Falls Grist Mill Ruins, Knechtel Feed Mill, Neustadt Mill, Orchardville Mill (Beatty Gristmill), Thornbury Mill, Traverston Mill, Walters Falls Mill, Welbeck Sawmill, Williamsford Mill
Haldiman County   Page 42
Caledonia Mill, Quance Mill
Huron County   Page 45
Benmiller (Gledhill Woolen Mill/ Pfrimmer Mill), Bluevale Mill, Folmar Windmill, Logan's Mill (Brussels Mill), Maitland Mill, Varna Mill
Norfolk County   Page 52
Backhouse Mill
Oxford County   Page 53
Otterville Mill, Plattsville Grist Mill, Thamesford Mill, Tillson Pea Mill
Waterloo Region   Page 58
American Standard Mill, Baechler Sawmill, Blackridge Mill, Dickson Mill, E.W.B. Snider (St. Jacobs Mill), Erb's Grist Mill, Ferrie Mill Ruins (Doon Mill), Galt Woolen Mill, Harrington Gristmill, Riverside Silk Mill, Sheave Tower/ Blair Mill, Turnbull Ruins, Wellesley Feed Mill

Wellington County Page 72
Aberfoyle Mill, Allan's Mill Ruins, Armstrong Mill, Arva Flourmills, Beatty Mill, Birge Mills, Eden Mills, Elora Mill, Goldie Mill Ruins, Grove's Mill, Hortop Mill, St. Andrew's Mill, Wissler's Mill
Wentworth County Page 86
Hammond Sawmill, Harris Woolen Mill Ruins

Central Ontario Region

Durham County Page 88
Brooklin Flourmill, Cream of Barley Mill, Tyrone Mill, Vanstone Mill
Haliburton County Page 92
Austin Saw Mill
Halton County Page 93
Barber's Mill, Beaumont Knitting Mill, Hilton Falls Mill Ruins, Williams Mill
Hamilton Region Page 98
Ancaster Old Mill, Cannon Knitting Mill, Darnley Gristmill Ruins, Fishers Mill Ruins (Gore Mills)
Hastings County Page 103
Cold Creek Lumber Mill, King's Mill, Latta Mill Ruins, Lonsdale Mill, Meyer's Mill, O'Hara Mill, Stockdale Gristmill
Kawartha Lakes Region Page 110
Lindsay Mill Ruins
Niagara Region Page 111
Ball's Falls Gristmill, Ball's Falls Woolen Mill Ruins, Dean Sawmill, Lybster Mill, Merritton Cotton Mill, Morningstar Mill, Secord Mill, Welland Mill
Northumberland County Page 121
Ball's Mill, Canton Mill, Molson Mill, Pratt's Mill, Purdy Mill
Ontario County Page 126
Port Perry Grain Elevator
Peel County Page 127
Alton Mill, Cataract Mill Ruins (Deagle Mill), Cheltenham Mill, Dods' Knitting Mill, Fowld's Mill, Hope Sawmill, Lang Mil, Needler's Mill
Peterborough County Page 132
Fould.s Mill. Hope Sawmill, Lang Mill, Needler's Mill

York County   Page 136
Bruce's Gristmill, Gooderham and Worts Distillery, Markham Cider Mill, Markham Saw Mill, Old Mill at Toronto, Roblin's Mill, Schomberg Feed Mill, Snider's Cider Mill, Stiver Mill, Todmorden Mills

Eastern Ontario Region
Frontenac County   Page 147
Babcock Mill, Bedford Mill, Bell Rock Mill, Chaffey's Lock Mill, Jackson's Mill (Glen Coe Mill), Kingston Woolen Mill, Lower Brewers Mill (Washburn Mill), Petworth Mill Ruins

Lanark County   Page 156
Boulton Brown Mill, Code's Mill, Collie Mill Ruins, Gillies Mill, Maberly Sawmill, Maple Leaf Mill, McArthur Mill, Merrickville Ruins, Mill of Kintail, Rosamond Mill, Thoburn Mill, Victoria Woolen Mill (Rosamond Mill 1), Wood's Mill

Leeds and Grenville County   Page 170
Delta Mill (Old Stone Mill), Island City Mill, Roddick Mill Ruins, Shepherd's Gristmill, Spencerville Mill, Windmill Lighthouse

Lennox and Addington County   Page 177
Hoopers Mill (Newburgh Mill), Thompson Paper Mill Ruins, Union Flour Mills Ruins

Ottawa-Carleton Region   Page 180
Watson's Mill (The Long Island Mill)

Perth County   Page 181
Adam's Mill (Glen Tay Mill)

Prince Edward County   Page 182
Chisholm Mills, Glenora Mill (Van Alstine Mill), Scott's Mill

Renfrew County   Page 185
Balaclava Mill, Bowe's Mill (Fraser Mill, Tay View Mill), Eganville Gristmill Ruins, McDougall Mill, Old Killaloe Mill

Stormont, Dundas and Glengarry County Pg 191
Asselstine Woolen Mill, Beach's Sawmill, Bellamy's Mill, Martintown Mill, Priest's Mill

Northern Ontario Region

Manitoulin County   Page 197
Manitowaning Roller Mills

Parry Sound Region Page 198
South River Grist Mill
Simcoe County Page 199
Baldwin Mill, Bell Gristmill, Coldwater Mill, Collingwood Gristmill, Collingwood Saw Mill, Hillsdale Mill, Marchmont Mill, Nicolston Gristmill, Sutton Mill, Udora Mill (Peers Grist Mill), Washago Grist Mill
Sudbury Region Page 210
Domtar Paper Mill

Self Guided Tours
Bruce County Tour (Half Day) Page 212
Grey County Tour (Half Day) Page 214
Cambridge Tour (Half Day) Page 216
Niagara Region Tour (Half Day) Page 218
Peterborough County Tour (Half Day) Page 220
Mississippi River Tour (Half Day) Page 222
Leeds and Grenville County Tour (Half Day) Page 223
Frontenac County Tour (Full Day) Page 225
Hastings County Tour (Half Day) Page 227
Lake Simcoe Tour (Full Day) Page 229

Index Page 232

How to use this Book

What is included in this book

For each of the more than 180 historical mills found in Ontario, we have included photographs as well as descriptive and statistical data.

Following is data included for each bridge:

Name: This is listed in bold type, and where there are other names, it is the common name or the name listed on an accompanying plaque.

Other Names: If the mill is known by other names, you will find them in brackets after the common name.

Region: The mills have been grouped into four regions to make it easier to plan your trips. You can see the mills in each region through the Table of Contents. The regions encompass the following counties:

Western: Brant, Bruce, Grey, Haldiman, Huron, Norfolk, Norwich, Oxford, Waterloo, Wellington and Wentworth.

Central: Durham, Haliburton, Halton, Hamilton, Hastings, Kawartha Lakes, Niagara, Northumberland, Ontario, Peel, Peterborough and York.

Eastern: Frontenac, Glengarry, Lanark, Leeds and Grenville, Lennox and Addington, Northumberland, Ottawa-Carleton, Perth, Prince Edward, Renfrew, and Stormont Dundas and Glengarry.

Northern: Manitoulin, Parry Sound, Simcoe and Sudbury

Type: The type of milling that was or is done is noted.

Location: The Nearest Settlement, Water Source and County are listed under this heading. These can be an aid in planning your trip and finding the building.

It is frustrating to go on an excursion to see something and not be able to find it. This book offers you multiple ways to ensure that doesn't happen.

Occasionally there is no water source and only the Nearest Settlement and County will be listed

When Built: The year the structure was built is shown if known.

Current Use: Very few of the mills are still actively milling, and this gives an idea of the current use.

Access: While almost all of the mills offer only reasonable exterior views, only a few offer interior access and this will be noted.

GPS Position: This is our recommended method. Enter the coordinates in a good GPS unit and it should take you right there. On rare occasions, you might find yourself directed to abandoned roads, so use common sense. The author visited all of these sites in a regular passenger vehicle.

Directions: Simple driving instructions are offered but GPS use is preferred.

History: A summary of the history of the mill is included although sometimes not a great deal is known.

Photography Tips: We offer a bit of advise on what we found that may offer interesting our unique opportunities for photography. Also have a look at our section on "Photographing Historic Mills".

Nearby Attractions: Generally this section lists the mills that are nearby, with a link to them. occasionally it lists other items of interest.

References: Links to websites of interest to this individual mill will be shown, especially if there is one dedicated to the mill.

Photographing Historic Mills

Some standard positions

Front: Taken to show the main entrance of the mill. This is often less than satisfying unless you can add interesting foreground elements such as flowers or artifacts.

3/4 view: Shows both the front and sides of the mill, and is often the most attractive.

Side view: Taken from a bank or from the river, this gives not only a nice view of the mill but usually allows for some interesting foreground elements.

Interior view: An image taken from the interior of the bridge will show some interesting structure as well as machinery but there is not a lot of available light. A tripod is important and HDR processing is helpful.

Landscape View: With the bridge smaller in the frame, you can introduce the habitat around it, particularly effective with colourful autumn foliage or with snow.

Details: Closer views will show interesting aspects of texture and weathering, old brick or wood. You can also find dramatic compositions in windows, doors and the mill race.

Reflections: Since most early mills were powered by water, you will usually find a river or millpond which will offer reflections of the mill.

Using HDR(High Dynamic Range)

HDR is a process where multiple images of varying exposure are combined to make one image.

It has a bad name with some people because many HDR images are super-saturated, a kind of digital age version of an Elvis painted on velvet. However, the process is actually about getting a full range of exposure with no burnt out highlights or blocked shadows.

This is an ideal processing solution for photographing Old Mills where you often have open light sky set against dark shadowed landscape and structure.

I use a series of three exposures at levels of -1 2/3, 0, +1 2/3, and this normally runs the full exposure range encountered. It is important to use a stable tripod.

One situation where you may need a larger series is shooting from within a mill and using the window to frame an outside scene. The dynamic range is huge and you will need to have a series with a much larger range.

There are a number of software programs you can use to combine these images including newer editions of Photoshop. I use Photomatix which I have found very versatile and easy to use.

Best times for photographing bridges

Mornings and evenings are generally the best times for outdoor photography but the use of HDR processing makes it easier even in bright direct light.

Although any season is good for mill photography, fall foliage included in a scene can be spectacular. In the winter, many photographers find their opportunities are limited but old mills make excellent subjects at that time of year.

Milling in Ontario

The first mills in Ontario were constructed as the first European settlers arrived. These mills were the lifeblood of the local economies, providing those early settlers with basic goods necessary for food, clothing and shelter, and offering an outlet for farmers to sell their goods. In fact mills were considered so important to new settlers that Britain used to send experienced millers to areas were there was new settlers.

Mills were generally within a day's wagon ride from the farms they serviced and it was natural that taverns, inns and commercial stores would spring up around the mills to accommodate these travelers.

Mills of the 19th Century could use such things as water, wind, horses and even humans to provide the energy needed to power mills. The overwhelming source in Ontario was water power and mills were usually built were the force of water was strong, often beside waterfalls. Waterwheels were first used.

When the water turned the wheel by pouring onto the top of the wheel, the wheel was said to be overshot and undershot when it entered at the bottom. Later most of these waterwheels were replaced by turbines which spun like a child's top and were much more efficient.

A major event in the life of many mills was the building of the railways which could provide them with less expensive transport for their raw materials and finished foods. Where the railway was built often determined whether a mill would survive or not, and often determined if the surrounding communities would flourish or wither away.

By the middle of the 20th century many mills found themselves in financial difficulties due to many factors such as economy of scale and ceased operations. While some lay abandoned, many were converted to other uses such as restaurants and commercial offices. Many of the smaller stone buildings have been renovated as private residences.

List of Mills

Western Ontario Region

Brant County
Apps Mill

Type: Gristmill
Location: Brantford, Whiteman's Creek, Brant County
When Built: 1841
Current Use: Abandoned
Access: Exterior only

GPS Location: N 43° 07.999' W 80° 22.599'
Directions: From Highway 403 Brantford, take Rest Acres Rd/ Highway 24 south for 3.2 km. and turn right onto Robinson. Rd. After about 800 m. you cross a bridge and the mill is a short distance on the left.

History: Built in 1841, it was actively operated until 1954. At that time Hurricane Hazel washed out the dam which supplied the mill with water and it was abandoned.

It was purchased by the Grand Valley Conservation Authority but at present the building is deemed unsafe.
Photography Tips:
The windows set off by the warm brown siding provide excellent photographic compositions.

Nearby Attractions: The St. George Mill is about a half hour drive.

German Woolen Mill Ruins

Type: Woolen Mill
Location: Glen Morris, Grand River, Brant County
When Built: 1867
Current Use: Ruins
Access: Public Access

GPS Location: N 43° 18.504' W 80° 33.559'

Directions: From the Village of Glen Morris, go north on Highway 24 (Brantford Highway) for about 1 km. Watch for a pull off on the left hand side. You will find a trail there that leads down toward the river and the abandoned mill.

History: The mill was built by Alva and Sydney German in 1867. It eventually closed due to competition and was used for a while as a lodge. It was later converted to a private residence but this was sold when a local railroad cut off the access road. The old building is said to be haunted. This may be due to that drowning death of a young girl while it was a mill and the murder of a guest when it was a lodge. The link below has further information.
http://hamiltonparanormal.com/german1.html

Photography Tips: There is a lot of foliage to make a photographer's life difficult. Look for a good view from near the mill race.

Nearby Attractions: The St. George Mill and Apps Mill are a short drive from here.

St. George Mill

Type: Gristmill
Location: St George, Brant County
When Built: 1871
Current Use: Commercial businesses
Access: Exterior views

GPS Location: N 43° 14.635' W 80° 15.374'
Directions: Found at 41 Main St. South in St. George

History: Built around 1871, it operated as a gristmill for many years, and in its later years as a feed mill. It has been renovated for commercial use.

Photography Tips: There is an elevated parking lot to the north of the mill which offers an excellent side view.

Nearby Attractions: Apps Mill is about 15 minutes drive from here.

Bruce County

Arranvale Mill

Type: Gristmill (?)
Location: Invermay, Sauble River, Bruce County
When Built: Not known
Current Use: Abandoned
Access: Good exterior views

GPS Location: N 44° 27.276' W 81° 08.835'
Directions:
From County Rd. 17 in Invermay, take Mill Rd. south for 1 km. and you will see it by the bridge on your left.

History: There was a Gristmill built by Luke Gardner in this area in about 1868. The current building doesn't look that old but we have no other information on it.

Photography Tips:
Good views from the road and the bridge area.

Nearby Attractions:
Fisher Grist Mill is a short drive nearby.

Fisher Grist Mill

Type: Gristmill
Location: Paisley, Saugeen River, Bruce County
When Built: Not Known
Current Use: Commercial
Access: Exterior only

GPS Location: N 44° 18.382' W 81° 16.435'
Directions: Found at the corner of Mill Dr. and Queen St. S. in Paisley

History: This mill has been renovated as a commercial business. Its build date is not known

Photography Tips:
The best view is from the other side of the river.

Nearby Attractions:
Stark's Mill is nearby in Paisley, and the McLure's Mill, Scone Mill and Pinkerton Mill are also a short drive.

McCullough Mill

Type: Feed Mill
Location: Allenford, Sauble River, Bruce County
When Built: Not known
Current Use: Storage
Access: Exterior views

GPS Location: N 44° 32.113' W 81° 10.655'
Directions: From the Town of Allenford turn south off County Rd 21 on Thomas St. and the mill is a short distance by the bridge.

History:
It was operated as a Feed Mill by the McCullough brothers until the late 1960s.

Photography Tips: There are good views from several spots but one of the best is from across the river by the bridge.

Nearby Attractions:
Arranvale Mill and Parkhead Mill are a short drive.

McClure's Mill

Type: Gristmill
Location: Chesley, North Saugeen River, Bruce County
When Built: 1881
Current Use: Warehouse
Access: Exterior views only

GPS Location: N 44° 17.886' W 81° 06.204'
Directions: From 1st Ave S/County Road 30 in the town of Chesley, take the 1st right onto 2 St SW, and go 700 m. to Thomas St. The mill is on this corner.

History:
Built as a gristmill by William Elliot in 1881. It presently is being used for storage.

Photography Tips: There are great views from all sides. Look for some views with reflections of the building on the millpond at the back.

Nearby Attractions:
The Stark Mill is nearby in the town. The Scone Mill is also close.

Mildmay Chopping Mill

Type: Feed Mill
Location: Mildmay, Witter's Pond, Bruce County
When Built: Ca. 1900
Current Use: Unused
Access: Exterior views

GPS Location: N 44° 02.216' W 81° 07.015'
Directions: From the Town of Mildmay, go north on Adam St off of County Rd 28. It is only a short distance.

History:
This mill operated to grind grain for cattle for many years. It is currently unused but the owner would like to renovate it.

Photography Tips:
There is a good wide view from the road.

Nearby Attractions:
The Fisher Grist Mill and Stark's Mill are nearby.

Parkhead Chopping Mill

Type: Feed Mill
Location: Parkhead, Water Source, Bruce County
GPS Location: N 44° 35.732' W 81° 09.829'
When Built: Not Known
Current Use: Abandoned
Access: Exterior Views

History:
We have little information on this mill. It was apparently operated as a chopping mill and water powered.

Getting There: Take Park Head Rd., west from County Rd. 10 north of Alvanley for about 2.7 km.

Photography Tips:
There is a trail that goes from the bridge on the opposite side of the creek which supports excellent views. It is not posted but may be on private property.

Pinkerton Mill

Type: Gristmill
Location: Pinkerton, Teeswater River, Bruce County
When Built: 1928
Current Use: May produce hydro
Access: Exterior views

GPS Location: N 44° 12.813' W 81° 16.144'
Directions: Found by the north side of County Rd. 15 in Pinkerton

History: The first gristmill at this site was built in the 1850s by David Pinkerton but was destroyed in a fire and re-built in 1896. The second mill was also destroyed by fire in 1928 and re-built with the present mill which was operated as a feed mill until 1999. The mill may continue as a producer of hydro.

Photography Tips: Wide views available as well as closer details.

Nearby Attractions: Stark's Mill, the Scone Mill and McLure's Mill are all nearby.

Scone Mill

Type: Gristmill
Location: Scone, North Saugeen River, Bruce County
When Built: 1856
Current Use: Abandoned
Access: Exterior views only

GPS Location: N 44° 18.317' W 81° 04.592'
Directions: Found on Bruce Road 10 just west of the Grey-Bruce Line Road in the village of Scone.

History: Built in 1856 along the Rocky Saugeen River and operated as a gristmill. It was renovated to hold an art gallery and bicycle shop but suffered severe damage in a flood in 2010 and is currently abandoned.

Photography Tips: The best view is from across the dam. The building is condemned and unsafe.

Nearby Attractions: McLure's Mill, Stark's Mill and Pinkerton Mill are all nearby.

Stark's Mill (Paisley City Roller Mills)

Type: Gristmill
Location: Paisley, Saugeen River, Bruce County
When Built: 1885
Current Use: Commercial business
Access: Exterior views

GPS Location: N 44° 18.024' W 81° 16.782'

Directions:
From Queen St S. (County Rd 3) in downtown Paisley, go west on Mill Dr. (County Rd 1) and you will find the mill on the right side after about 1 km.

History:
Built in 1885 by James Stark, it replaced an earlier mill that burned. It operated as a gristmill and feed mill until 1972. it currently houses a commercial business.

Photography Tips:
This is a gorgeous building with the red window frames against the blue-grey siding. There are good views from three sides but the long view from the west side is one of the best.

Nearby Attractions:
The McLure's Mill, Scone Mill and Pinkerton Mill are nearby.

Bruce County

Grey County

Ayton Mill

Type: Gristmill
Location: Ayton, South Saugeen River, Grey County
When Built: 1864
Current Use: Private
Access: Exterior views only

GPS Location: N 44° 03.156' W 80° 55.678'
Directions:
Found on Arthur St. (County Rd. 3) off of County Rd 9 in Ayton.

History: Built in 1864 by Thomas Robertson, the gristmill was water powered and it still produces power for the hydro grid. It is now a private residence.

Photography Tips:
There is a great view which includes the river in the foreground from the bridge.

Nearby Attractions: The Neustadt Mill, as well as the Ferguson Gristmill and the Knechtel Feed Mill, are a short drive.

Ferguson Gristmill

Type: Gristmill
Location: Durham, Rocky Saugeen River, Grey County
When Built: 1857
Current Use: Private Residence
Access: Exterior views only

GPS Location: N 44° 13.749' W 80° 49.999'
Directions: Go north from Durham on highway 6 till you cross the Rocky Saugeen River after 5.7 km, and you will see the mill on the left side.

History: Built by Alex Ferguson in 1857 on the Rocky Saugeen River, and operated as a gristmill. It is a beautiful stone building that has been renovated as a private residence.
Photography Tips:
There is a gorgeous view from the bridge which shows the river in the foreground.

Nearby Attractions: The Welbeck Sawmill, Traverston Mill, and Knechtel Feed Mill are all a short drive.

Flesherton Mill

Type: Woolen Mill
Location: Flesherton, Millpond, Grey County
When Built: 1931
Current Use: Private residence
Access: Poor exterior views only.

GPS Location: N 44° 15.759' W 80° 33.476'
Directions: Found on Harold Best Parkway off Grey Road 4 in Flesherton

History:
Probably built by William Flesher around 1931 to replace the original mill (Ca. 1865) that burned.

Photography Tips:
The present owner has trees growing around the building and there is no open shot available without permission.

Nearby Attractions:
The Holstein Mill and Orchardville Mill are nearby.

Herb Miller Saw Mill

Type: Sawmill
Location: Rockford, Grey County
When Built: ca. 1920
Current Use: Exhibit
Access: Exterior views

GPS Location: N 44° 31.272' W 80° 56.484'
Directions: From Highway 6/10 at Rockford, just south of Owen Sound, take Grey Road 18 east about 2 km to #102599.
History:
A 78' X 40', timber framed, board sided, steel roofed building housing a circular saw mill typical of many simple, small scale operations found along township concession and side roads, circa 1920. Moved 2006 (From Website)

Photography Tips:
At present, there are just exterior views but they may be developing an interior exhibit.

Nearby Attractions:
Inglis Falls Mill Remains is just minutes away.

Holstein Mill

Type: Feed Mill
Location: Holstein, Mill Pond from Saugeen River, Grey County
When Built: 1918
Current Use: Feed Mill
Access: Exterior views

GPS Location: N 44° 03.701' W 80° 45.529'
Directions: Found in the Village of Holstein beside Grey Rd 109

History:
The original mill on this site was built by W.T. Petre in 1876 and was water powered. This mill was destroyed by a fire in 1918 and the present mill replaced it.

Photography Tips: Not the most photogenic of buildings but there is an excellent view from the road.

Nearby Attractions:
Orchardville Mill and Flesherton Mill are a short drive.

Inglis Falls Grist Mill Ruins

Type: Gristmill
Location: Rockwood, Sydenham River, Grey County
When Built: 1862
Current Use: Ruins
Access: Easy access

GPS Location: N 44° 31.583' W 80° 56.072'
Directions: From Highway 6/10 just south of Owen Sound, go west on Grey Road 18 for 1.3 km. and turn right on Inglis Falls Rd. After 450 m. there is a right turn to Falls Road which will bring you shortly to the Falls.

History: In 1845 Peter Inglis purchased a gristmill at this site and in 1862 he replaced it with a four storey that operated as a gristmill. The mill was in operation until it was destroyed by a fire in 1945. The only remains are the millers home and some artifacts. The area is presently the Inglis Falls Conservation Area.

Photography Tips: While there are no ruins remaining to photograph, the whole area, especially the waterfall, will give you some great opportunities.

Nearby Attractions:
The Herb Sawyer Sawmill is just a short distance west on Grey Road 18.

Knechtel Feed Mill

Type: Feed Mill
Location: Durham, Saugeen River, Grey County
When Built: ca. 1900?
Current Use: Commercial
Access: Exterior views only

GPS Location: N 44° 10.667' W 80° 49.008'
Directions: Found at George St. East, one block north and east of Durham's only traffic light on Highway 6.

History: We have little historical information available other than it is known to have operated as a feed mill for decades before being renovated for commercial use.

Photography Tips: Found in a wide open setting by the Saugeen River, it offers a dam which can be worked into the foreground, as well as some nice floral elements at the side.

Nearby Attractions: The Ferguson Gristmill is only a few kilometers north of Durham.

Neustadt Mill

Type: Grain mill
Location: Neustadt, Saugeen River, Grey County
When Built: 1857
Current Use: Antique Store
Access: Exterior and interior with permission

GPS Location: N 44° 04.521' W 81° 00.179'
Directions: Found at 566 Mill St. in Neustadt

History: Built in 1857 and operated as a grain mill until 1990. Some charred beams in the interior are a remnant of a 1947 fire.

Photography Tips: Good long views from the parking lot or the dam behind. Also look for antique items on the porch.

Nearby Attractions:
Neustadt is also the birthplace of Canada's 13th Prime Minister, John Diefenbaker, and the home can be seen. Ayton Mill is a short drive.

Orchardville Mill (Beatty Gristmill)

Type: Gristmill
Location: Orchardville, Mill Pond, Grey County
When Built: Ca. 1880
Current Use: Private Residence
Access: Exterior views

GPS Location: N 44° 03.975' W 80° 47.546'
Directions:
From Highway 6, south of Durham, take Orchardville Side road, just south of Side road 35, and park at the end. The mill is just up the road.

History: Orchardville was a thriving community from 1865 until the end of that century. The mill was probably built around 1880. The settlement rapidly declined around the beginning of the 20th century but the mill has survived and been renovated as a private residence.

Photography Tips:
The property is private but their are good open views from the road.

Nearby Attractions: The Ferguson Gristmill and Holstein Mill are a short drive.

Thornbury Mill

Type: Mill Type
Location: Thornbury, Beaver River, Grey County
GPS Location: N 44° 33.686' W 80° 27.173'
When Built: Not Known
Current Use: Restaurant
Access: Exterior views

History: Perhaps built about 1880, it took advantage of the water power supplied by the Beaver River. It is currently a restaurant.

Getting There:
Located on the corner of Bruce St. S. and Bridge St. in Thornbury.

Photography Tips:
There are interesting views from the bridge which include the dam.

Nearby Attractions:
The Flesherton Mill is about 40 minutes drive although it is not easy to see and photograph.

Traverston Mill

Type: Gristmill
Location: Traverston, Rocky Saugeen River, Grey County
When Built: 1870
Current Use: Private residence
Access: Exterior views only

GPS Location: N 44° 16.463' W 80° 44.514'

Directions: Found on Traverston Rd, between Concession Rd 8 and Grey Road 12 as you cross an iron bridge.

History: Built in 1870 and operated as a gristmill till 1955, the Traverston Mill has been renovated as a private residence.

Photography Tips: There is a great view from the iron bridge which includes the river and gorge in the foreground.

Nearby Attractions:
The Ferguson Gristmill and Welbeck Sawmill are nearby.

Walters Falls Mill

Type: Sawmill
Location: Walters Falls, Walter's Creek, Grey County
When Built: 1890 (rebuilt after a fire in 1984)
Current Use: probably abandoned
Access: Exterior views

GPS Location: N 44° 29.333' W 80° 42.7'
Directions: In the village of Walters Falls, go north on Front St., off of Victoria St. (Grey Road 29). At the end of the road is the Falls Inn and the mill is beside it.

History:
John Walter built the first sawmill here in 1851. This mill operated until 1890, when it was destroyed by fire and another mill built to replace it. I have seen this current mill described as a woolen mill and a gristmill, but most sources say it is a sawmill.

Photography Tips:
There are excellent views on all sides. The back in particular is impressive.

Nearby Attractions:
The Mill at Inglis Falls is about a 40 minute drive.

Welbeck Sawmill

Type: Sawmill
Location: Welbeck, Mill pond, Grey County

When Built: 1984
Current Use: Exhibit and retail outlet
Access: Good interior and exterior views

GPS Location: N 44° 16.525' W 80° 53.540'
Directions: From Highway 6 north of Durham, go east on Welbeck Rd. for about 3.2 km and you will see the mill on the south side.

History:
The present building is a modern replacement for a mill lost to a fire in 1966. It was completed in 1984.

Photography Tips: A great place for photographers, offering both interior and exterior views as well as interesting artifacts. The red waterwheel is only for show but offers a bonus element.

Nearby Attractions: The Williamsford Mill, Traverston Mill and Ferguson Gristmill are all nearby.

Williamsford Mill

Grey County

Type: Gristmill
Location: Williamsford, North Saugeen River, Grey County
When Built: 1858
Current Use: Restaurant and bookstore
Access: Good exterior views

GPS Location: N 44° 22.666' W 80° 52.285'
Directions: Found on Highway 6 in Williamsford

History: The mill was built by Adam Elliot in 1858 and operated as a gristmill and later as a feed mill. It ceased milling operations in the early 1970s although it continues to produce hydro power.

At one point this power was used for a marijuana grow operation but it has since been converted to a bookstore and restaurant.

Photography Tips: Good exterior views from all sides but particularly the back which includes the mill pond and millrace.

Nearby Attractions: The Welbeck Sawmill is nearby.

Haldiman County

Caledonia Mill

Type: Mill Type
Location: Caledonia, Grand River, Haldiman County
When Built: 1853
Current Use: Heritage designated, no present use
Access: Exterior only

GPS Location: N 43° 04.294' W 79° 57.462'
Directions:
Located at 146 Forfar St. West in the town of Caledonia.

History: Built about 1853 by James Little and called Little Mills at that time. At various times it has been called the Balmoral Mill and the Grand River Mill. The Shirra Mill which was on the other side of the river, was operated by the same owners from 1929 to 1966. The Shirra Mill burnt to the ground in 1969.

The mill is currently owned by the Caledonia Old Mill Corp., a non-profit organization.

Photography Tips:
There are interesting shots available from across the river, you will need a longer lens. I used a 70-200mm.
Nearby Attractions:
Apps Mill is about 40 minutes drive

Quance Mill

Type: Gristmill
Location: Delhi, Big Creek, Haldiman County
When Built: 1913
Current Use: Exhibit
Access: Exterior views and interior with permission

GPS Location: N 42° 51.322' W 80° 31.69'
Directions: Found at 200 Talbot St. in Delhi

History: Built in 1913, it operated as a gristmill until 1970. There were plans for its demolition in 2006 but a local service group adopted and renovated it.

Photography Tips: Close views as well as longer from across the dam and river

Nearby Attractions: The Tillson Pea Mill, Otterville Mill and Backhouse Mill are near by.

Huron County

Benmiller (Gledhill Woolen Mill/ Pfrimmer Mill)

Type: Gristmill and Woolen Mill
Location: Goderich, Maitland River, Huron County
When Built: Ca 1850
Current Use: Country Inn
Access: Exterior views

GPS Location: N 43° 43.320' W 81° 37.620'

Directions:
Found at 81175 Benmiller Road near Goderich. Benmiller Road runs just off Lonesboro Rd (County Rd. 15)

History: The buildings were built near Goderich in the 1850s by three brothers appropriately named Miller. In 1857 Thomas Gledhill purchased and operated the Woolen Mill. The Woolen Mill was operated until 1964 and the gristmill until the early part of the 1970s. It has been renovated as a luxury country retreat.

Photography Tips: The bridge behind the gristmill offers a great view with the river in the foreground.

Nearby Attractions:
The Folmar Windmill and Varna Mill are about a half hour drive.

Bluevale Mill

Type: Sawmill
Location: Bluevale, Little Maitland River, Huron County
When Built: 1909
Current Use: Commercial equipment sales
Access: Exterior views

GPS Location: N 43° 51.234' W 81° 15.060'
Directions: Found in Bluevale, just off Clyde Line.

History:
One of a number of mills which were built along the Maitland River. This one was built in 1909 to replace a mill that was destroyed by fire and operated as a sawmill.

Photography Tips:
There are excellent views from across the river. Look for close up details as well.

Nearby Attractions:
The Maitland Mill and Logan's Mill are only a short drive.

Folmar Windmill

Type: Sawmill and Gristmill
Location: Bayfield, Huron County
When Built: Ca 1990
Current Use: Exhibit

Access: Exterior views only. It has been closed for tourist visits to the interior although many web pages still say otherwise.

GPS Location: N 43° 34.908' W 81° 39.666'
Directions: Located off of the Bluewater Highway (County Rd. 21), about 4 km east on Bayfield River Rd.

History: Modeled after a famous Dutch windmill called the Arend, the Folmar Windmill is North America's only wind driven saw mill. Located near Bayfield, Ontario. Although it is not a historical building, it has been included because it is interesting.

Photography Tips: The open fields surrounding it make for some long distance views isolating it.

Nearby Attractions: The Varna Mill is only a short drive.

Logan's Mill (Brussels Mill)

Type: Gristmill
Location: Brussels, Maitland River, Huron County
When Built: 1911

Huron County

Current Use: Abandoned
Access: Exterior only

GPS Location: N 43° 44.428' W 81° 14.800'
Directions: From County Rd 16 in Brussels, go south on Turnberry St, and then another left on Mill St. which takes you to the mill shortly.

History: This is the third mill on the site. The first was built by William and James Vanstone in 1859, and it was destroyed by fire in 1871. The second was also lost to a fire in 1911. The present building was built by John Logan in 1911 and was in operation until 1967. It is presently owned by the Maitland Valley Conservation Area.

Photography Tips: The walkway across the dam offers some excellent set up point. There is also an excellent view from across the river upstream. There is also a good front view with the old water turbine in the foreground.

Nearby Attractions: The Maitland Mill and the Bluevale Mill are only a short drive.

Maitland Mill

Type: Gristmill
Location: Gorrie, Maitland River, Huron County
When Built: 1856
Current Use: Abandoned
Access: Exterior only

GPS Location: N 43° 52.268' W 81° 06.353'
Directions: In the village of Gorrie, go east on Edward St., off Victoria St. (County Rd 28) and the mill is a short distance on the left, or continue north on Victoria St. (County Rd 28) past Edward St. to the entrance to Gorrie Park on the right.

History:
The mill was built by the seven Leach brothers in 1856 as a gristmill and operated until 1962. It was then purchased by the Maitland Valley Conservation Area and currently sits abandoned.

Photography Tips:
There are excellent wide shots available. Additionally look at the east side for interesting images which include the mill race and the varied colored rock in the foundation.

Nearby Attractions: Bluevale Mill and Logan's Mill are nearby.

Varna Mill

Type: Feed mill
Location: Varna, Huron County
When Built: ca.1890
Current Use: Pet supply store
Access: Exterior views and an interesting interior.

GPS Location: N 43° 32.100' W 81° 35.76'
Directions: Found at 1 Mill St in Varna (the main intersection)

History:
The building was originally a haberdashery but was converted to a feed mill. It currently operates as a pet supply business.

Photography Tips:
It doesn't offer a typical old mill look due to commercial signage but there are easy exterior views available.

Nearby Attractions:
The Folmar Windmill is nearby.

Norfolk County

Backhouse Mill

Type: Gristmill
Location: Port Rowan, Otter Creek, Norfolk County
When Built: 1798
Current Use: Exhibit
Access: Excellent exterior views.

GPS Location: N 42° 38.986' W 80° 28.107'
Directions: From Highway 59, turn left on Concession Rd. 2 and you will see the signs for the Backus Mill Conservation area about 2.5 km. on the left.

History: Built in 1798 by the Backhouse family and operated until the 1950s, it was purchased by Long Point Conservation Area in 1956. It is part of an exhibit of buildings of a heritage village.

Photography Tips: The red painted flume running to the mill makes a great foreground element.

Nearby Attractions: The other heritage buildings make a great day long visit combined with a family picnic.

Oxford County

Otterville Mill

Type: Gristmill
Location: Otterville, Otter River, Norwich County
When Built: 1845
Current Use: Exhibit
Access: Easy exterior views

GPS Location: N 42° 55.569' W 80° 36.337'
Directions: The Otterville Mill is located on the south side of Main Street West, west of Dover Street, east of Church Street and east of the Otter River, in Mill Park.

History:
The mill was built in 1845 by Edward Bullock and operated as a gristmill run on water power. It is currently maintained as an exhibit by the South Norwich Historical Society.

Photography Tips:
As well as good wide views from the front and sides, there is a longer shot from below, across the dam and river.

Nearby Attractions: The Tillson Pea Mill, Quance Mill and Backhouse Mill are only a short drive.

Plattsville Grist Mill

Type: Gristmill
Location: Plattsville, Oxford County
When Built: 1888
Current Use: Agricultural sales
Access: Exterior views

GPS Location: N 43° 18.250' W 80° 37.151'
Directions:
Found at 24 Hume St. in Plattsville

History:
Initially a gristmill built on 1888, it is currently a feed mill.

Photography Tips:
You can get all of the building from the back of their parking lot although it may not be the most photogenic of subjects.

Nearby Attractions:
The Erb's Gristmill is about a half hour drive.

Thamesford Mill

Type: Feed mill
Location: Thamesford, Thames River, Oxford County
When Built: 1898
Current Use: Abandoned
Access: Exterior views only

GPS Location: N 43° 03.605' W 80° 59.809'
Directions:
Found on Milton St., near the intersection of Dundas St. E in Thamesford.

History:
There was a mill built on this site in 1851 by James Finkle which was destroyed by fire. The present mill replaced it in 1898 and operated until 1997. It is currently abandoned. As of 2013, it was being demolished.

Photography Tips: Good views from in front at Milton St. as well as an excellent view across the river.

Nearby Attractions: Harrington Gristmill is nearby.

Tillson Pea Mill

Type: Pea and Barley Mill (later a Gristmill)
Location: Tillsonburg, Big Otter Creek, Oxford County
When Built: 1878
Current Use: Restaurant
Access: Exterior views

GPS Location: N 42° 51.360' W 80° 43.467'
Directions:
Found at 20 John Pound Rd in Tillsonburg

History: Built by E.D. Tillson, Tillsonburg's first mayor, in 1878, and operated as a Pea and Barley Mill. From 1955 to 1972 it operated as a gristmill. It has been renovated to use as a restaurant.

Photography Tips:
One of the nicest views is the front from across the road but you need to choose a time when the parking is not full of cars. There are some nice building details on the east side.

Nearby Attractions:
The Quance Mill and Otterville Mill are nearby.

Waterloo Region

American Standard Mill

Type: At times, flour, liquor, cotton and wool
Location: Cambridge, Speed River, Waterloo Region
When Built: 1847
Current Use: Condominiums
Access: Private but excellent exterior views

GPS Location: N 43° 25.877' W 80° 18.648'
Directions: Found at 19 Guelph Ave. in Cambridge

History: At one time owned by Jacob Hespeler, founder of Village of Hespeler which is now part of Cambridge. It has had various uses including flour and wool milling.
In 1913 Stamped Enamel began making sinks there, and where eventually bought out by American Standard in 1969. Its latest life is condominium units due to open in 2011.

Photography Tips:
There is a walkway across the river which provides great views. Look for panoramas involving the dam.

Nearby Attractions:
The Dickson Mill, Galt Woolen Mill, and Riverside Silk Mill are all nearby in Cambridge, as is the Turnbull Ruins.

Baechler Sawmill

Type: Sawmill
Location: Kitchener (Doon), Waterloo Region
When Built: Ca. 1914
Current Use: Museum exhibit
Access: Public access

GPS Location: N 43° 24.054' W 80° 26.255'
Directions:
10 Huron Rd. at Homer Watson Boulevard, Kitchener; 3 km north of Hwy 401 at Interchange 275

History: Operated as a sawmill in Waterloo Region and gifted to the museum where it is an exhibit in the Doon Pioneer Village.

I don't have the original build date.

Photography Tips: Not a particularly photogenic building but easy to set up on all sides. There is some interesting equipment inside.

Nearby Attractions: The Doon Pioneer Village has about 18 historic buildings of the era around 1914. The Ferrie Mill Ruins are a few minutes drive from here.

Blackbridge Mill

Type: Gristmill
Location: Cambridge, Waterloo Region
When Built: 1856
Current Use: An Inn
Access: Private but easy views from the road.

GPS Location: N 43° 27.009' W 80° 17.710'
Directions: Found in Cambridge at 4860 Townline Road.

History: A gristmill located near Puslinch Lake near Guelph, it was built by Peter Holm in 1856. In the 1940's it operated as a feed mill and was renovated as a private residence in 1978. Most recently it has been made into an Inn, the Blackbridge Mill Inn .

Photography Tips:
Easy to set up from the road for exterior shots.

Nearby Attractions: A short drive from Blair Mill/Sheave Tower as well as the Dickson Mill, Turnbull Mill Ruins, Galt Woolen Mill, and the Riverside Silk Mill.

Dickson Mill

Type: Gristmill
Location: Cambridge, Grand River, Waterloo Region
When Built: 1842
Current Use: Restaurant
Access: Public access

GPS Location: N 43° 21.779' W 80° 19.098'
Directions: Found at 4 Park Hill Rd. W. in Cambridge

History: A five storey mill built in 1842 and operated for about 100 years. Most recently, it has been renovated as a restaurant.

Photography Tips: Excellent views of the mill and dam from across the river.

Nearby Attractions: The Turnbull Mill ruins are across the road and the Galt Woolen Mill and the Riverside Silk Mill are a short walk.

E.W.B. Snider (St. Jacobs Mill)

Type: Gristmill
Location: St. Jacobs, Water Source, Waterloo Region
When Built: 1851
Current Use: Commercial businesses
Access: Public access

GPS Location: N 43° 32.426' W 80° 33.219'
Directions: Found at 1441 King St. North in St. Jacobs

History: The mill was purchased by E.W.B. Snider in 1871. In 1875 he introduced the Steel Rolling system used in Europe, the first Canadian operation to use it.

Waterloo Region

Photography Tips: There are exterior views from the parking lot and from across the road.

Nearby Attractions: Erb's Grist Mill is a short drive.

Erb's Grist Mill

Type: Gristmill
Location: Waterloo, Silver Lake, Waterloo Region
When Built: 1998 (Replica of a mill built in 1816)
Current Use: Exhibit
Access: Easy exterior views

GPS Location: N 43° 27.926' W 80° 31.579'
Directions: On the corner of Caroline St. N., and Dupont St. W. in Waterloo

History: This is a 1998 replica of a a gristmill built in 1816. The original was built by Abraham Erb, Waterloo's first settler, and was demolished in 1927.

Photography Tips: It is easy to get full frame shots from the bank of the lake in front of the mill.

Nearby Attractions: The St. Jacobs Mill is a short drive.

Ferrie Mill Ruins (Doon Mill)

Type: Flour mill
Location: Kitchener, Grand River, Waterloo Region
When Built: 1839
Current Use: Ruins
Access: Public access

GPS Location: N 43° 23.651' W 80° 24.975'
Directions: From Highway 401 at Kitchener, take exit 275 Homer Watson Blvd. North and turn right on Conestoga College Blvd. after 500 m. After another 500 m. turn left on Doon Valley Dr. Follow Doon Valley Rd. (it becomes Pinnacle Dr.) for a km to Old Mill Rd. and the ruins are about 200 m. on the right.

History: The ruins of a flour mill built by Adam Ferrie Jr. in 1839.

Photography Tips: You can walk anywhere on the site and close up views may be best.

Nearby Attractions: Baechler Sawmill and Sheave Tower/Blair Mill are close by.

Galt Woolen Mill

Type: Woolen Mill
Location: Cambridge, Grand River, Waterloo Region
When Built: Ca. 1850
Current Use: Offices
Access: Private but excellent exterior views

GPS Location: N 43° 21.417' W 80° 18.923'
Directions: Located at 36 Water St. South in Cambridge.

History: Built by Isaac Sours in Galt (now Cambridge) about 1850. It was purchased by Tiger Brand in 1881 and they operated from there until 1904. it has been renovated to house offices.

Photography Tips: One of the best views is from across the river which shows the water intake structure.

Nearby Attractions: Dickson Mill, Turnbull Mill Ruins and Riverside Silk Mill are within walking distance.

Harrington Gristmill

Type: Gristmill
Location: Harrington, Millpond off Thames River, Waterloo Region When Built: 1846
Current Use: Exhibit
Access: Exterior only

GPS Location: N 43°14.475' W 80°59.517'
Directions: Found in Harrington just off 96 Rd. (County Rd. 28 on Victoria St.

History: Built as a gristmill by a United Empire Loyalist named D.L. Demorest. It initially operated by an overshot waterwheel but this was replaced a water driven turbine in the 1880s. It operated from 1846 until 1966 with a couple of interruptions due to a 1924 fire, and dam breaks in 1903 and 1949.

Photography Tips: There is an interesting view across the river near the dam although you need to carefully pick a spot due to trees.

Nearby Attractions: The Thamesford Mill is only a short drive.

Riverside Silk Mill

Type: Textile Mill
Location: Cambridge, Grand River, Waterloo Region
When Built: 1919
Current Use: School for Architecture
Access: Portions of the interior are accessible, easy exterior views

GPS Location: N 43° 21.458' W 80° 19.008'

Directions: Located at 7 Melville St. South in Cambridge

History: Built on the Grand River in Cambridge (then Galt) by the brothers D. and E. McCormick in 1919. Operations continued with various owners until 1975. The building currently houses the Waterloo School for Architecture.

Photography Tips: There is a parking lot on the south side which provides good views.

Nearby Attractions: The Dickson Mill, Galt Woolen Mill and the Turnbull Mill ruins are all within walking distance.

Sheave Tower/Blair Mill

Type: Gristmill
Location: Blair, Blair Creek, Waterloo Region
When Built: 1876 (Sheave Tower) 1846 (Blair Mill)
Current Use: Exhibit
Access: Public access (Sheave Tower), Private (Blair Mill)

GPS Location: N 43° 22.955' W 80° 23.364'

Directions: Located in Blair on Old Mill Rd., between Blair Rd. and Meadow Creek Lane.

History:
The Sheave Tower is a unique structure used to generate energy and transfer it to the Blair Mill to use in their operation. The mill was originally named the Carlisle Mill and was built in 1846. It is still in operation.

Photography Tips:
The Blair Creek makes an excellent foreground for the Sheave Tower. The Blair Mill is a more difficult subject due to foliage but there are decent views from the road.

Nearby Attractions: The Cambridge Mills are a short drive. These are the Dickson Mill, the Galt Woolen Mill, the Turnbull Mill Ruins and the Riverside Silk Mill.

Turnbull Ruins

Type: Woolen Mill
Location: Cambridge, Grand River, Waterloo Region

Waterloo Region

When Built: 1897
Current Use: Ruins
Access: Public Access

GPS Location: N 43° 21.779' W 80° 19.098'
Directions: Found at the corner of Park Hill Rd East and Water St. North in Cambridge

History: Charles and John Turnbull built a mill at this site in 1897, replacing one that had burned. The mill was in operation until 1972.

Photography Tips: You can walk among the ruins for interesting details. The mill race running through the middle can be an effective element.

Nearby Attractions: The Dickson Mill is across the road and the Galt Woolen Mill and the Riverside Silk Mill are only a short walk.

Wellesley Feed Mill

Waterloo Region

Type: Flour Mill
Location: Wellesley, Waterloo Region
When Built: 1856
Current Use: Abandoned
Access: Exterior views

GPS Location: N 43° 29.535' W 80° 45.870'
Directions: Found on Haldiman Rd. in the village of Wellesley

History:
Built in 1856 by the Doering brothers, it operated as a flour mill. Originally two stories, a third was added in 1910 as well as an addition on the front.

Photography Tips:
Good exterior views from many sides as well as interesting details.

Nearby Attractions:
The E.W.B. Snider Mill in St. Jacobs is about a half hour drive.

Waterloo Region

Wellington County

Aberfoyle Mill

Type: Gristmill
Location: Aberfoyle, Pond, Wellington County
When Built: 1859
Current Use: Restaurant
Access: Exterior easy, interior if you are using the restaurant

GPS Location: N 43° 28.105' W 80° 08.631'
Directions: Aberfoyle is on Wellington Rd 46, and the mill is at the south end of the village.

History: The mill was built by George McLean, a Scottish immigrant and functioned as a gristmill until the 1920s. In the 1960s it was renovated as a restaurant.

Photography Tips: The exterior is easy to photograph from the parking area.

Nearby Attractions:
The Goldie Mill Ruins in Guelph is about a half hour drive.

Allan's Mill Ruins

Type: Gristmill
Location: Guelph, Speed River, Wellington County
When Built: Ca. 1832
Current Use: Ruins
Access: Exterior views

GPS Location: N 43° 32.830' W 80° 14.677'
Directions: At the south east corner of MacDonnell St. and Woolwich, you will find the remnants of Allan's Mill with a historical plaque.

History: A five storey Stone Structure was built by William Allan around 1832 to replace a wooden mill, known as the Canada Mill, which was originally on the site. The mill suffered a number of fires in later years and there is only a small bit of ruins there today.

Photography Tips: The artifacts make a nice combination with the stone remnants. The graffiti is annoying.

Nearby Attractions: The much more impressive Goldie Mill Ruins are only a short distance nearby.

Armstrong Mill

Type: Mill Type
Location: Armstrong Mills, Wellington County
When Built: 1856
Current Use: Private residence
Access: Private but good exterior views from the road.

GPS Location: N 43° 37.773' W 80° 15.608'

Directions: From Guelph, take Wellington County Rd. 124 north for about 5 km., and turn left on Jones Baseline. Another 4 km. brings you to Armstrong Mills. Turn left on Mill St. and you will see the mill after a short drive.

History: The Armstrong Mill was constructed by John and Mary Scott in 1856 and was in use until 1950 due to the bursting of the dam. The realist painter Ken Danby purchased it and restored it as a private home and studio, and it appears as a subject in some of his paintings.

Photography Tips: If you walk along the road, you will find a couple of excellent views. Plan on using a medium lens, I used a 24-70mm

Nearby Attractions:
Birge Mill, Hortop Mill and the Goldie Mill Ruins are a short drive.

Arva Flourmills

Type: Flour mill
Location: Arva, Medway Creek, Wellington County
When Built: 1819
Current Use: Continues to operate
Access: Interior with permission

GPS Location: N 43° 03.169' W 81° 17.687'
Directions: Found at 2042 Elgin St. in Arva, near London

History:
Built in 1819 and still in operation, Arva Flour Mill operated initially on water power. This was supplemented by partial use of electrical power around 1919.

Photography Tips: From near the mill pond, you can get a wide view of the building.

Nearby Attractions:
The Thamesford Mill is about a half hour drive.

Beatty Mill

Type: Various
Location: Fergus, Grand River, Wellington County
When Built: 1878
Current Use: Farmer's Market
Access: Public access

GPS Location: N 43° 42.298' W 80° 22.521'
Directions: Found by the bridge over the Grand River on St. David St. in Fergus.

History: Built in 1878 in the town of Fergus, Ontario, it is currently the Fergus market but started out as a foundry. The Beatty Brothers who owned it were famous for being against the "evils" of drink, dancing and flirtatious behavior and were able to bend the town laws to their will for many years. They also seemed to pay very low wages, and were big time polluters of the river. (From an article by Pat Mestern)

Photography Tips: There is a walkway across the river which provides some excellent wide views.

Nearby Attractions: Groves Mills is on the other side of the bridge.

Birge Mills

Type: Gristmill
Location: Birge Mills, Lutterill's Creek, Wellington County
When Built: 1880
Current Use: Private Residence
Access: Private but long views from the road.

Wellington County

GPS Location: N 43° 39.958' W 80° 15.544'
Directions: From Guelph, take Eramosa Rd. (County Rd 29 for 5.2 km. and turn left on Wellington Rd. 29. After 4.7 km. turn right on side road 20 and after 1.5 km., left on 3rd Line. After 1.4 km. you will see the mill on the right hand side.

History: Built in 1880 and operated as a gristmill by John Birge and Nicholas Lynett. It was later operated as a feed mill and ceased operations in 1991. It has been renovated as a private residence.

Photography Tips: There is no public access but there are views from the road. I used a 400 mm lens.

Nearby Attractions: Hortop Mill and Armstrong Mill are a short drive.

Eden Mills

Type: Gristmill
Location: Eden Mills, Wellington County
When Built: 1842

Wellington County

Current Use: Private residence
Access: Private with easy exterior views

GPS Location: N 43° 34.702' W 80° 08.820'
Directions: Located at the corner of York and Barden Streets in Eden Mills
History: The initial dam and mill in this site was built in 1842 by two brothers names Krib. This seems to have gone through many changes through the years with it ceasing operations in 1947. Some of the remains where used in the private residence shown in the attached image. There is also a water wheel remaining.

Photography Tips: Good views of the mill and pond are available from the road.

Nearby Attractions: Not far from the Harris Woolen Mill Ruins

Elora Mill

Type: Mill Type
Location: Elora, Grand River, Wellington County
When Built: 1859
Current Use: Inn and Restaurant

Access: Public access
GPS Location: N 43° 40.817' W 80° 25.867'
Directions: Located at 77 Mill St. West in Elora.
History:
J. Fraser owned a mill at this site which had been built in 1850, and after it burned, the present mill was built in 1859. It is six stories tall and an imposing structure in an impressive setting. The mill operated until 1974 and was then converted to an Inn and restaurant.

Photography Tips: From across the river you can, with care, work yourself into a position that overlooks the waterfall and the inn. This will include the small island called the Tooth of Time.
The whole area is a dream for photographers with old buildings, remnants of mill runs and the Elora Gorge.

Nearby Attractions: Wissler's Mill, St. Andrew's Mill, Beatty Mill and Grove's Mill are all a short distance away.

Goldie Mill Ruins

Type: Flour Mill
Location: Guelph, Speed River, Wellington County

Wellington County

When Built: 1866
Current Use: Ruins (Used for public venues)
Access: Public access

GPS Location: N 43° 33.016' W 80° 15.245'
Directions: Located on Cardigan St. in Guelph between Norwich St. E. and London Rd. E.

History: Built in 1866 in Guelph by James Goldie at the site of a burnt out mill. It was destroyed by fire in 1953.

Photography Tips: You can enter the mill from the back for interior shots.

Nearby Attractions: Armstrong Mill is a short drive from here.

Grove's Mill

Type: Gristmill
Location: Fergus, Grand River, Wellington County

When Built: 1850
Current Use: Pub
Access: Easy exterior views

GPS Location: N 43° 42.341' W 80° 22.645'
Directions: Found at 170 St David St S., in Fergus.

History: Originally built as a tannery, it was converted to a gristmill around 1880 by Dr. Abraham Groves. It also provided the first electrical power to Fergus.

Photography Tips: There is a good wide view available from across the bridge.

Nearby Attractions: The Beatty Mill (Fergus Market) is across the street.

Hortop Mill

Type: Gristmill
Location: Everton, Eramosa River, Wellington County

When Built: 1865
Current Use: Abandoned
Access: Exterior only

GPS Location: N 43° 39.695' W 80° 09.180'
Directions: Found on Evert St. (7th Line) a few hundred meters south of the Village of Everton

History: Constructed in 1865, it was purchased by Henry Hortop Jr. in 1874. In 1966 it was purchased by the Grand River Conservation Authority and is closed to the public at present.

Photography Tips: There are easy exterior views. Look for a grinding stone near the front.

Nearby Attractions: The Harris Woolen Mill Ruins and the Birge Mill are both a short drive from here.

St. Andrew's Mill

Type: Gristmill
Location: Fergus, Grand River, Wellington County

Wellington County

When Built: 1856
Current Use: Condominiums
Access: Private but easy exterior views

GPS Location: N 43° 42.642' W 80° 22.128'
Directions: Found in Fergus on St. Andrew's St., between Scotland St. and Herrick St. N.

History: Built by Robert Steele in 1856 in Fergus, it has had a number of names, including the Monkland Mill and the Walkley Mill. The mill was in operation until 1993, and has recently been converted to condominiums

Photography Tips: There are public paths across from the mill which provide good views of the mill and dam. Look for parking near the bridge.

Nearby Attractions: Beatty Mill and Grove's Mill are nearby.

Wissler's Mill

Type: Gristmill
Location: Elora, Irvine Creek, Wellington County

When Built: 1852
Current Use: Private Residence
Access: Exterior views

GPS Location: N 43° 41.6' W 80° 26.683'
Directions: Found at Woolwich St. West, near Geddes St. in Elora

History: Built in about 1852, Wissler's Mill was a grist mill that is situated by the Salem Bridge near Elora, Ontario. Like many Ontario mills, it has suffered some calamities. It was struck by lightning in 1899, losing most of a wall and was gutted in a fire in the 1920's but was re-built. It ceased operation in 1965. Subsequently it was converted to a private residence.

Photography Tips: You can get shots from the bridge. If you receive permission, there are also good views from across the creek.

Nearby Attractions: The Elora Mill is only a short drive.

Wentworth County

Hammond Sawmill

Type: Sawmill
Location: Rockton, Wentworth County
When Built: Not known
Current Use: Exhibit
Access: Public

GPS Location: N 43° 19.197' W 80° 08.656'
Directions: Located at 1049 Kirkwall Road (Regional Road # 552), Rockton, in the Westfield Heritage Village

History: This is a typical sawmill that could be found throughout Ontario at one time. They were often run part time only, doing jobs for local businesses and farms as needed.

Photography Tips: Easy exterior views

Nearby Attractions:
The Harris Woolen Mill ruins are nearby and the mill in St. George is about 20 minutes drive from here.

Harris Woolen Mill Ruins

Type: Woolen Mill
Location: Rockton, Wentworth County
When Built: 1884
Current Use: Ruins
Access: Public access

GPS Location: N 43°36.755' W 80° 08.867'
Directions: From the town of Rockton, go south off Highway 7 (Alma St.) on Falls St. S., and you will see the entrance to Rockwood Conservation area a short distance to your right.

History: Built in 1884 by John Harris to replace his wooden mill that was destroyed by fire. It was purchased by the Grand River Conservation Authority in 1958. After a fire in 1967, the ruins are what remains today.

Photography Tips: The Rockwood Falls are beside the mill ruins and a wide lens is necessary to include them.

Nearby Attractions: Hammond Sawmill is nearby.

Central Ontario Region

Durham County

Brooklin Flourmill

Type: Flourmill
Location: Brooklin, Lynde Creek, Durham Region
When Built: 1848
Current Use: Montessori School
Access: Exterior views

GPS Location: N 43° 57.385' W 78° 57.545'
Directions: Located at 25 Cassels Road East in Brooklin

History: Built in 1848 by brothers John and Robert Campbell, it replaced a mill built in 1840 which was destroyed by lightning. It operated as a mill until about 1991, and in 2002 it became home to a Montessori School.

Photography Tips: There is an open view in front and to the left near the creek.

Nearby Attractions: The Tyrone Mill is only a short drive.

Cream of Barley Mill

Type: Gristmill
Location: Bowmanville, Soper Creek, Durham County
When Built: 1904
Current Use: Visual Arts Center
Access: Good exterior views

GPS Location: N 43° 54.108' W 78° 40.404'
Directions: Located at 143 Simpson Ave. in Bowmanville

History: Timothy Soper built a gristmill in 1825 on Soper Creek in the present town of Bowmanville. It was purchased in 1886 by John MacKay, known as "The Barley King of Canada". It burned in 1904 and was replaced with the present building. The name Cream of Barley was after the breakfast cereal made here, popular in World War 1.
 The operation ended in the 1950s and was acquired by the Town of Bowmanville. It is presently used as a visual arts centre.

Photography Tips: Easy exterior views which you can add to with foreground elements like flowers.

Nearby Attractions: The Vanstone Mill is only a short drive

Tyrone Mill

Type: Gristmill and sawmill
Location: Tyrone, Lynde Creek, Durham Region
When Built: 1846
Current Use: Commercial
Access: Easy exterior views

GPS Location: N 44° 0.479' W 78° 43.29'
Directions: Take the Liberty Street exit on from the 401 at Bowmanville and continue north to the town of Tyrone. The mill is found on Tyrone Road.

History: Built in 1848, it has operated as a Flour mill, as well as a lumber mill and the production of apple cider. It is currently a country store.

Photography Tips: The best views are from the front and side. The building houses an antique woodworking shop.

Nearby Attractions: The Brooklin Flour Mill is a short drive.

Vanstone Mill

Type: Gristmill
Location: Bowmanville, Bowmanville River, Durham County
When Built: 1850
Current Use: Commercial business
Access: Exterior views

GPS Location: N 43° 54.746' W 78° 41.384'
Directions: Found at 116 King St. West in Bowmanville

History: Originally a mill was managed on this site by John Burk around 1805. Samuel Vanstone took over the present mill in about 1856 and it operated as a family business until 1975.

Photography Tips: One of the best views is from across the river.

Nearby Attractions: Less than 5 minutes drive from the Cream of Barley Mill

Haliburton County

Austin Saw Mill

Type: Sawmill
Location: Kinmount, Burnt River, Haliburton County
When Built: 1942
Current Use: Exhibit
Access: Easy exterior views

GPS Location: N 44° 46.878' W 78° 39.084'
Directions: Easily found in the town of Kinmount on Highway 121 along the Burnt River

History: The present mill was constructed in the mid 1940s after the previous mill built in the 1908 burned along with most of the town. The bottom portion was rebuilt and the upper portion was from a mill moved from elsewhere. This water powered sawmill operating until the 1970s

Photography Tips: Excellent exterior views as well as from across the river.

Nearby Attractions: The nearest mill is the Lindsay Mill Ruins about an hours drive

Halton County

Barber's Mill

Type: Woolen Mill
Location: Georgetown, Credit River, Halton County
When Built: 1823
Current Use: Ruins
Access: Exterior views, interior posted

GPS Location: N 43° 39.078' W 79° 55.495'
Directions: Found at the north end of Mill St in Georgetown (Halton Hills) beside the Credit River.

History: The Barber Mill was built in 1823 near present day Georgetown, Ontario. In 1954 it was purchased by the Barber brothers who converted it from a woolen mill to produce rag paper. The property has been deserted for some years, with plans for development seemingly on hold. I have seen images of the inside which are very interesting but would not now be possible without trespassing.

Photography Tips: Excellent exterior view from the bridge to the north.

Nearby Attractions:
The Beaumont Knitting Mill is a short drive.

Beaumont Knitting Mill

Type: Knitting Mill
Location: Halton Hills, Halton County
When Built: Ca. 1872
Current Use: Commercial Businesses
Access: Exterior only

GPS Location: N 43° 40.603' W 79° 55.719'
Directions: Located on Main St. just north of Joseph St. in the Village of Glen Williams (Halton Hills)

History:
The historic Plaque says:
"Town of Halton Hills-Beaumont Knitting Mill
Joseph Tweedle ran a saw mill on this site in the 1860's. The present building was built circa 1872 by Richard Hurst and purchased in 1882 by Samuel Beaumont. The structure operated as a knitting mill until 1972."

Photography Tips:
There are wide views from the parking areas on both sides.

Nearby Attractions:
The Barber Mill is a short drive.

Hilton Falls Mill Ruins

Type: Sawmill
Location: Campbellville , Sixteen Mile Creek, Halton County
When Built: Ca. 1856
Current Use: Ruins
Access: Open and easy to view

GPS Location: N 43° 30.56' W 79° 58.75'
Directions: Located at Hilton Falls Conservation Area located on Campbellville Rd, just of the Highway 401. The trail into the ruins is about a half hour walk.

History: The mill was built by an Ancaster doctor named George Park around 1856. It used a 40 foot water wheel and was destroyed in a fire in 1860.

Photography Tips: The Hilton Falls is just beside the ruins and provides an excellent element in photographs. You can make your way to creek level for some great views.

Nearby Attractions: Not far from the Barber Mill.

Williams Mill

Type: Multiple uses
Location: Glen Williams, Water Source, Halton County
When Built: Ca.1850
Current Use: Artists' studios and galleries
Access: Exterior views

GPS Location: N 43° 40.589' W 79° 55.587'
Directions: Located at 515 Main Street in Glen Williams (Halton Hills)

History: These three 19th century buildings have included a gristmill, sawmill and flour mill. They have been renovated to house an interesting collection of artist studios and galleries. The first building, a saw mill, was built by Benajah Williams and his sons, Joel and Charles, about 1825. The oldest of the remaining buildings probably dates to the 1850s.

Photography Tips: The center court near the steps offers interesting views. In season, there are flower beds which can be included in the foreground.

Nearby Attractions: The Beaumont Knitting Mill and the Barber Mill are a short drive.

Hamilton Region

Ancaster Old Mill

Type: Gristmill
Location: Ancaster, Ancaster Creek, Hamilton Regional Municipality
When Built: 1863
Current Use: Restaurant
Access: Excellent exterior views

GPS Location: N 43° 13.993' W 79° 58.467'
Directions: The mill is located at 548 Old Dundas Rs. in Ancaster. From Wilson St. EW., go north and make a left on Montgomery Dr. and take the next left onto Old Dundas Rd. The mill is only a short distance on the left.

History: Harris and Alonzo Egleston built the gristmill at the present site in 1863. It replaced two earlier mills here, one of which burnt in 1812 and the second in 1854.

Photography Tips: The mill can be photographed from three sides and their is a waterfall/mill race at the back which provides interesting detail. Also have a look at the upper falls near the south part of the building.

Nearby Attractions: The Darnley Gristmill Ruins are only a short drive.

Cannon Knitting Mill

Type: Knitting Mill
Location: Hamilton, Hamilton Regional Municipality
When Built: Ca. 1860
Current Use: Abandoned
Access: Good exterior views

GPS Location: N 43° 15.546' W 79° 51.732'
Directions: Located at the corner of Mary Street and Cannon St. East in Hamilton

History: This building is said to have been built in about 1860 and operated as a knitting mill for many years. Rumor has it that it has been sold to a developer who will turn it into condos. If so, it would have a lot of pluses, close to the city centre, a park out behind and solid construction.

Photography Tips: This abandoned building has a lot of interesting texture. Look for details and wide views.

Nearby Attractions: The Ancaster Old Mill and the Darnley Gristmill Ruins are a short drive.

Darnley Gristmill Ruins

Type: Gristmill
Location: Greensville, Spencer Creek, Hamilton Regional Municipality

Hamilton Region

When Built: 1813
Current Use: Ruins
Access: Good views although the interior is posted

GPS Location: N 43° 16.704' W 80° 0.224'
Directions: From Highway 403 in Hamilton, take Exit 74 and go north on Highway 6. Turn left on Highway 5 and go 7 km and make another left on Brock Rd.. Turn right on Old Brock Rd., which turns into Crooks Hollow Rd. After 1 km, you will come to the ruins on your right.

History: James Crook built a gristmill here in 1813, naming it after Lord Darnley. The area evolved into an industrial centre by 1829. In 1885 it was damaged by an explosion which killed two men but was repaired. In 1934 the mill was destroyed by a fire.

Photography Tips: There are many good vantage points for images including details. You can also visit the Darnley Cascade behind it.

Nearby Attractions: The Ancaster Old Mill is a short drive.

Fishers Mill Ruins (Gore Mills)

Type: Paper Mill
Location: Dundas, Spencer Cr., Hamilton Regional Municipality
When Built: Ca. 1863
Current Use: Ruins
Access: Easy views

GPS Location: N 43° 16.370' W 79° 58.339'
Directions: Found in Dundas at King St. W. just west of Bond St. at the edge of the escarpment. There is a pull off just past the bridge and a trail to the mill ruins.

History: John Fisher bought the Gore Mill in 1863 and used it to make newsprint, carpet, felt and paper. It operated until 1929 when it was torn down.

Photography Tips: Look for the remains of the arch of the mill race. You will probably need a tripod.

Nearby Attractions: The Darnley Gristmill Ruins and the Ancaster Old Mill are nearby.

Hastings County

Cold Creek Lumber Mill

Type: Lumber Mill
Location: Frankford, Cold Creek, Hastings County
When Built: Not known
Current Use: Abandoned
Access: Good exterior views

GPS Location: N 44° 11.702' W 77° 37.654'
Directions: Found across from the gristmill at 1914 Stockdale Rd. in the town of Frankford.

History:
I have no information on this mill. I noticed it while visiting the Stockdale Gristmill.

Photography Tips:
Easy exterior views from across the creek or from the bridge.

Nearby Attractions:
The Stockdale Mill is across the creek.

King's Mill

Type: Gristmill
Location: Wellman, Hoards Creek, Hastings County
When Built: About 1840
Current Use: Unused (Conservation Area)
Access: Exterior access

GPS Location: N 44° 19.929' W 77° 37.729'
Directions: From the Village of Wellman, take County Rd. 19 south for 1.3 km, the mill is on the left side.

History: The mill was built around 1840 and operated as a gristmill until 1963. It was purchased by the Lower Trent Conservation Authority.

Photography Tips:
This is a gem of a building with the red roof and woodwork setting off the stone construction. It can be photographed from multiple positions. Look for artifacts at the north side.

Nearby Attractions:
Stockdale Mill and Fowld's Mill are only a short drive.
Latta Mill Ruins

Type: Gristmill
Location: Latta, Moira River, Hastings County
When Built: About 1833
Current Use: Ruins
Access: Public Access

GPS Location: N 44° 18.066' W 77° 20.410'
Directions: In the small settlement of Latta, the mill ruins are found by the river on Hoskin Rd.

History:
The site of the mill was purchased by John Latta in 1833. Little else is known of it's history although it was apparently demolished about 1995.

Photography Tips:
If you get down to the river, you will see the remains of the mill race by the dam.

Nearby Attractions:
Chisholm's Mill is only a short drive.

Lonsdale Mill

Type: Gristmill
Location: Lonsdale, Salmon River, Hastings County
When Built: 1842
Current Use: Private residence
Access: Exterior only

GPS Location: N 44° 16.448' W 77° 07.566'
Directions: From the village of Lonsdale, go south on Marysville Rd to the bridge over the Salmon River, the mill is to the east.

History: I don't have a lot of information on this mill. Built in 1842, it is now a private residence.

Photography Tips: As it is private property, you can only take images from the road. You will need to move up and down it to find the few good spots, but they can include the dam.

Nearby Attractions:
Chisholm's Mill is about 40 minutes drive from here.

Meyer's Mill

Type: Gristmill
Location: Belleville, Moira River, Hastings County
When Built: 1792 (Original)
Current Use: Private
Access: Exterior Views

GPS Location: N 44° 10.270' W 77° 22.960'
Directions: Located at 54 Station St. in Belleville.

History: Built by Captain John Meyer's, a famous Loyalist soldier, and one of the original builder of the present town of Belleville. He purchased this property in 1789 and built the
original mill in 1792.

Photography Tips: Views from the side which include the river can be exceptional.

Nearby Attractions: Chisholm's Mill is about 30 minutes drive as is the Latta Mill Ruins.

O'Hara Mill

Type: Sawmill
Location: Madoc, Deer Creek, Hastings County
When Built: About 1830
Current Use: Conservation area exhibit
Access: Public access

GPS Location: N 44° 30.996' W 77° 31.499'
Directions: From the town of Madoc, take the Trans-Canada Highway (Highway 7) west to O'Hara Rd and go north for about 2 km. and turn left
on Mills Rd.

History: This sawmill was built on this site about 1830 by Robert Taylor and was active until at least 1908. The water wheel is a recent addition. In 2011, the dam was being re-built.

Photography Tips: You can get a nice full frame shot which includes the dam and mill with the water wheel.

Nearby Attractions: King's Mill is about a half hour drive away.

Stockdale Gristmill

Type: Gristmill and Cider Mill
Location: Frankford, Cold Creek, Hastings County
When Built: 1867 (Gristmill) 1923 (Cider Mill)
Current Use: Restaurant
Access: Good exterior views

GPS Location: N 44° 11.702' W 77° 37.654'
Directions: Found at 1914 Stockdale Rd. in the town of Frankford.

History: Built in 1867 and operated as a gristmill, the red building was added in 1923 and used as a Cider Mill. It is currently a restaurant.

Photography Tips: There are long views from the bridge and from in front.

Nearby Attractions: There is a very picturesque abandoned Lumber Mill on the other side of the creek.

Hastings County

Kawartha Lakes Region

Lindsay Mill Ruins

Type: Flour mill and Lumber mill
Location: Lindsay, Trent-Severn Waterway, Kawartha Lakes
When Built: 1869
Current Use: Ruins
Access: Public access

GPS Location: N 44° 21.401' W 78° 43.914'
Directions: Located at Kent St. East in the Town of Lindsay

History: Built in 1869, they have operated as a flour mill and lumber mill. In 1978 they were destroyed in a fire and the ruins have been incorporated in a public park.

Photography Tips: It is easy to find a wealth of interesting angles and textures. Be sure to poke your camera through the bar covered windows for some interior shots.

Nearby Attractions:
The Port Perry Grain Elevator is about 45 minutes drive.

Niagara Region

Ball's Falls Gristmill

Type: Gristmill
Location: Vineland, Twenty Mile Creek, Niagara Regional Municipality
When Built: 1809
Current Use: Exhibit
Access: Good exterior views

GPS Location: N 43° 08.001' W 79° 22.946'
Directions: Take Exit 57 off QEW (Niagara) and go south on Regional Rd 24 through Vineland. After about 6 km. you will see a sign for Ball's Falls Conservation Area (Sixth Ave). Parking is less than a km. on the left. The Gristmill is across the road beside the lower falls.

History: John and George Ball were awarded this land as soldiers loyal to the British in the American Revolution. They built this five story grist mill at the lower of two waterfalls in 1809. The Niagara Conservation Authority purchased the property in 1962.

Photography Tips: There are excellent interior views, perhaps seen best when the few trees around the building have lost their leaves.

Nearby Attractions: The two waterfalls, Balls Falls Upper and Lower are wonderful. The ruins of the Balls Woolen Mill is near the Upper Falls.

Ball's Falls Woolen Mill Ruins

Type: Woolen Mill
Location: Vineland, Twenty Mile Creek, Niagara Regional Municipality
When Built: Ca.1840
Current Use: Ruins
Access: Good views

GPS Location: N 43° 08.001' W 79° 22.946'
Directions: Take Exit 57 off QEW (Niagara) and go south on Regional Rd 24 through Vineland. After about 6 km. you will see a sign for Ball's Falls Conservation Area (Sixth Ave).

Parking is less than a km. on the left. Follow the trail upstream on the side across from the parking lot and you will find the ruins before you reach the upper falls.

History: John and George Ball were awarded this land as soldiers loyal to the British in the American Revolution. They built a five story grist mill at the lower of two waterfalls in 1809 and added a woollen mill near the Upper Falls in about 1840. The Niagara Conservation Authority purchased the property in 1962.

Photography Tips: You can use the remains of a window to frame interesting views, especially in the fall

Nearby Attractions: The two waterfalls, Balls Falls Upper and Lower are wonderful. The Balls Falls Gristmill still stands near the Lower Falls.

Dean Sawmill

Type: Sawmill
Location: Wainfleet, Niagara Region

When Built: 1883
Current Use: Exhibit
Access: Good exterior views

GPS Location: N 42° 55.242' W 79° 22.645'
Directions: Located at the Marshville Heritage Village near Wainfleet.

History: The mill was built by Cyrus Dean in 1883 and operated nearby to its present site until the mid 1960s. The water tower provides water to run the operation under steam power. (My thanks to Art Dean, the great grandson of the original owner for this information).

Photography Tips: It has an interesting water tower you will want to include. Take a wide lens.

Nearby Attractions: Morningstar Mill is about 30 minutes drive.

Lybster Mill

Niagara Region

Type: Cotton Mill
Location: St. Catharines, Second Canal, Niagara Regional Municipality
When Built: 1860
Current Use: Restaurant
Access: Good exterior views

GPS Location: N 43° 7.980' W 79° 11.964'
Directions: Located at Merritt St. in St. Catharines

History: Built in 1860 in St. Catharines as a Cotton Mill, and powered by water from a system of weirs on the Second Canal. It is currently a restaurant.

Photography Tips: Wide views are available from across the street and in the parking lot.

Nearby Attractions: Across the street from the Old Merritton Cotton Mill

Merritton Cotton Mill

Type: Cotton Mill
Location: St. Catharines, Second Canal, Niagara Regional Municipality
When Built: 1885
Current Use: Restaurant
Access: Exterior views

GPS Location: N 43° 7.980' W 79° 11.964'
Directions: Located on Merritt St., near Townline Rd in St. Catharines

History: The Beaver Cotton Mill was built in 1857 on this site and was destroyed by fire in 1881. The present building replaced it in 1885. It was not in use during the Great Depression and was renovated as a restaurant in 2001.

Photography Tips: Good exterior views from the parking lot.

Nearby Attractions: The Lybster Mill is across the road.

Morningstar Mill

Type: Gristmill
Location: Decew Falls, Twelve Mile Creek, Niagara Regional
When Built: 1872
Current Use: Museum
Access: Good exterior and interior at times

GPS Location: N 43° 6.617' W 79° 15.816'
Directions: To reach the Morningstar Mill, Highway QEW (Niagara) take exit 49 southeast and merge onto King's Hwy 406.Take the St. David's Rd West/County Rd-71 exit, merge onto St David's Rd. and turn left at Merrittville Hwy. Take the 1st right onto Decew Rd. There is a parking lot and it is well signed.

History: (From the Mill Website) The gristmill was built in 1872 on land owned by Robert Chappel to process wheat, oats, barley and rye. It was constructed of native stone quarried from Beaverdams Creek to form the mill pond. The mill stones (flinty burr stones) originally came to Canada from the LaFerte fields of France and were brought over as ballast on ships planning to take back logs for sale in France. In 1875, the City of St Catharines Water Works Commission purchased property at DeCew Falls and constructed dams across Beaverdams Creek, interfering with the water supply to the mill. As a consequence, in 1878, the City of St Catharines was compelled to purchase the property from Chappel. This was the beginning of a long relationship between the City and the site that is locally known as "Morningstar Mill."

The City proceeded to lease the mill to a number of millers. Ellis and Drake ran the mill for a time and their names appear on the original sign, under layers of paint. By the early 1880s the third Welland Canal had been completed and resulted in an abundance of water to power the mill. The City sold the property to Wilson Morningstar in 1883, who in turn leased it to Charles Knoll.

Around 1892, the interior of the Mill was destroyed by fire but the original stone structure remained intact. Morningstar, assisted by his brother Wallace, rebuilt the mill installing new equipment acquired in Toronto from the Greey Company.

Wilson Morningstar operated the mill until his death in the mill by heart attack in1933. The water-powered turbine seized shortly thereafter and the mill was abandoned. Morningstar's widow, Emma, sold the property in 1941 to Ontario Hydro who repaired the turbine building. In 1961 Hydro leased the property to the City of St Catharines, and the next year Mountain Mills Museum was opened with Donald Robson, Morningstar's grandson, as the curator.

Ontario Hydro declared the property surplus and the City purchased the mill site in 1989. In 1992 the volunteer group "Friends of Morningstar Mill" was established and they began to restore and then operate the mill as an operating gristmill. At the start of the restoration project, much of the machinery and stones were as Morningstar had left them in 1933.

Photography Tips: There are great views as well as close up details to be found. Look for a view from across the mill pond for some excellent reflections.

Nearby Attractions: The Decew Falls at the site is interesting and the St. Catharines mills of Merriton and Lybster are a short drive.

Secord Mill

Type: Gristmill
Location: Niagara-on-the-Lake, Four Mile Creek, Niagara Regional Municipality
When Built: 1783
Current Use: Private residence
Access: Exterior only

GPS Location: N 43° 09.144' W 79° 06.256'
Directions: Found at 137 Four Mile Creek Rd, St. Davids

History: The government built the mill in 1783 and it was initially worked by Peter Secord, father of the Canadian heroine, Laura Secord. His nephew David bought the property in 1799. The Four

Mile Creek supplied power for a couple of mills although it is quite small today.

Photography Tips: There are exterior views from the front and sides. It is private property.

Nearby Attractions: The Old Merriton Cotton Mill and Lybster Mill are nearby in St. Catharines

Welland Mill

Type: Gristmill
Location: Thorold, Second Welland Canal, Niagara Regional Municipality
When Built: 1846
Current Use: Housing and commercial business
Access: Exterior views

GPS Location: N 43° 7.560' W 79° 12.180'
Directions: Found at 20 Pine Street North in Thorold

History: Built in 1846 by Jacob Keefer in present day Thorold, it made use of the 2nd Welland Canal for both shipping and power to operate. It ceased production in the 1930s and was used for storage until recently being renovated for Affordable Housing

Photography Tips: Good views from across the street and the parking lot.

Nearby Attractions: The Lybster Mill and the Old Merriton Cotton Mill are only a short drive.

Northumberland County

Ball's Mill

Type: Carding Mill and then Flourmill
Location: Baltimore, Baltimore Creek, Northumberland County
When Built: 1846
Current Use: Private
Access: Exterior only

GPS Location: N 44° 2.028' W 78° 8.778'
Directions: From the town of Baltimore, go north on County Rd. 45 and veer left on Harwood Rd. The mill is less than a km. on the left.

History: After being built as a carding mill in 1846, it was purchased by John Ball in 1884 and operated as a Flour mill. It manufactured Shurflake Flour, renowned for it's quality

Photography Tips: There are excellent front views. The road passes a few feet from the side which offers some interesting opportunities.

Nearby Attractions: Pratt's Mill is only a short drive from here.

Canton Mill

Type: Gristmill
Location: Canton, Ganaraska River, Northumberland County
When Built: Probably about 1880
Current Use: Private offices
Access: Exterior views only

GPS Location: N 44° 0.054' W 78° 21.138'
Directions: From Highway 401 near Port Hope, take exit 461 north on County Rd 2, and continue onto County Rd. 10. Canton is about 4.5 km. from Highway 401

History: I have no information on this mill

Photography Tips:
View from the front with a set up on the road is the only available not on private property.

Nearby Attractions:
The Molson Mill, Pratt's Mill and Ball's Mill are all a short drive.

Molson Mill

Type: Gristmill
Location: Cobourg, Ganaraska River, Northumberland County
When Built: About 1850
Current Use: Art School
Access: Exterior views

GPS Location: N 43° 57.939' W 78° 17.686'
Directions: From Molson St. (County Rd. 70) take Cavan St. south and make a left on Old Cavan St. The mill is at the end of the road.

History: Built about 1850 in Cobourg by Thomas Molson, a member of the famous Brewing family, it was operated as a gristmill. It currently is occupied by an arts school.

Photography Tips: Gorgeous exterior views are available from all sides. The green painted exterior is striking.

Nearby Attractions:
The Canton Mill is less than half hour drive.

Pratt's Mill

Type: Gristmill
Location: Cobourg, River, Northumberland County
When Built: 1850's
Current Use: Restaurant
Access: Exterior views

GPS Location: N 43° 58.517' W 78° 10.998'
Directions: Found in the town of Cobourg at 990 Ontario St.

History: Built in the 1850's by Ebenezer Perry and initially known as Perry's Mill, it was sold to about 1889 to Alexander Pratt, and the Pratt family operated it until 1986. It is currently a restaurant.

Photography Tips: The parking lot and area at the front provide good views.

Nearby Attractions: Ball's Mill, Canton Mill and Molson Mill are a short drive.

Purdy Mill

Type: Perhaps a sawmill
Location: Castleton, Northumberland County
When Built: Probably before 1880
Current Use: Abandoned
Access: Exterior views

GPS Location: N 44° 05.075' W 77° 56.281'
Directions: Found on the main road (Percy St.) at the small town of Castleton.

History: I haven't found any information on the history of this mill. There is mention of a mill built in 1795 in Castleton but this mill is certainly much younger than that.

Photography Tips: Excellent view from across the highway

Nearby Attractions: Ball's Mill is a short drive.

Ontario County

Port Perry Grain Elevator

Type: Feed Mill
Location: Port Perry, Ontario County
When Built: 1875
Current Use: Commercial
Access: Exterior

GPS Location: N 44° 6.324' W 78° 55.446'
Directions: Found at Water St. near Queen St. in Port Perry

History:
Built in 1875 by George Currie, it operated as a feed Mill in Port Perry. It ceased operation in 1979 and was renovated for commercial use. It has survived a half dozen fires.

Photography Tips:
From across the road at the front, there are various wide views.

Nearby Attractions:
It is a short drive from the Tyrone Mill

Peel County

Alton Mill

Type: Woolen Mill
Location: Alton (Caledon), Shaw's Creek, Peel County
When Built: 1881
Current Use: Commercial businesses
Access: Exterior views

GPS Location: N 43° 51.525' W 80° 04.269'
Directions: Located at 1402 Queen St. West in Alton (Caledon)

History:
From the Ontario Heritage Plaque
"The Alton Mill was established on the bank of Shaw's Creek in 1881 by local industrialist and philanthropist William Algie. Known as the Beaver Knitting Mill, it was renowned across Canada for its production of fleece-lined long underwear. Although it miraculously survived the great Alton flood of 1889, the mill was struck by a disastrous fire in 1908, which reduced the original three-and-a-half storey limestone building to its present two storeys.

In 1935 Frederick N. Stubbs of the Western Rubber Co. converted the mill to manufacture rubber products including balloons for Disney and condoms for Canadian troops during the Second World War. The mill remained in operation until 1982 and was the longest- running water -powered mill on the upper Credit River system."

Photography Tips: There are some great sculptures which can be used as foreground elements.

Nearby Attractions:Dod's Knitting Mill is a short drive.

Cataract Mill Ruins (Deagle Mill)

Type: Gristmill
Location: Cataract, Credit River, Peel County
When Built: Ca.1890
Current Use: Ruins
Access: Easy exterior, difficult interior

GPS Location: N 43° 49.256' W 80° 1.320'

Directions: From the village of Cataract, go south on Cataract Rd for a short distance to the entrance of Forks of the Credit Provincial Park. A five minute walk on the trail will bring you to the falls and the mill ruins.

History: John Deagle built the mill near the Cataract Falls on the Credit River, probably around 1890. It was turned into a hydro-electric plant in 1899 and operated until 1923.

Photography Tips: This is a difficult place to photograph as it is down in a steep gorge. You can get a view from the railway side. You can also descend from the other side with the aid of a line of short trees but use caution as the ground is steep and loose.

Nearby Attractions: The Schomberg Feed Mill is a short drive.

Cheltenham Mill

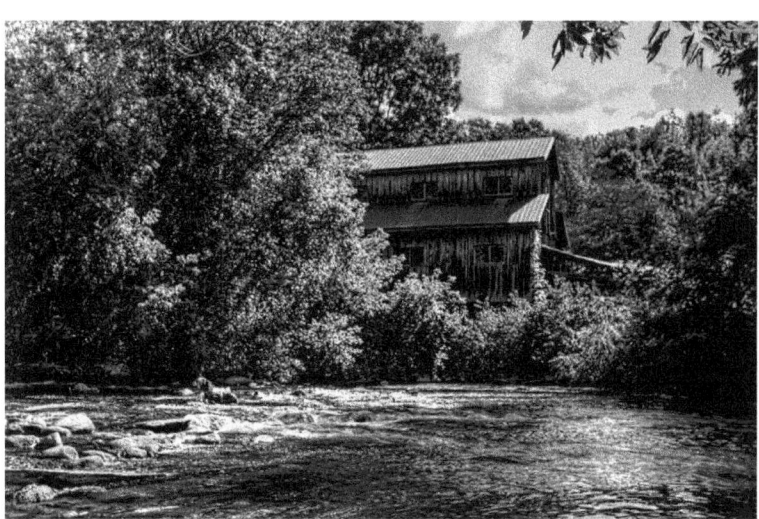

Type: Gristmill
Location: Cheltenham, Credit River, Peel County
When Built: 1847?
Current Use: Abandoned

Access: Exterior views from across the river.

GPS Location: N 43° 44.868' W 79° 55.350'
Directions: From Creditview Road in Cheltenham, take Mill St South for about 450 m. until a sharp bend in the road. The mill is on the left on the other side of the river.

History: Charles Haines, the original settler of the area, built a wooden gristmill along the Credit River in 1847. It is not certain that this is the mill that is referred to but we have not located any information otherwise.

Photography Tips: You can see the mill from the road but it is doubtful if a reasonable image can be taken. The best view is from the bank of the river opposite the mill but this is posted and you will need to get permission.

Nearby Attractions: The Beaumont Knitting Mill and Williams Mill are a short drive.

Dods' Knitting Mill

Type: Knitting Mill
Location: Alton (Caledon), Shaw's Creek, Peel County
When Built: 1881
Current Use: Inn and Restaurant
Access: Good exterior views

GPS Location: N 43° 51.378' W 80° 04.549'
Directions: Located on Bridge St. in the Town of Alton

History: Built along Shaw's Creek in Alton in 1881 by Benjamin Ward, and operated as a knitting mill. A 1917 fire initiated extensive renovations. It ceased operations in 1965 and has been renovated into a top notch Inn

Photography Tips: Excellent exterior views available which can incorporate the waterfall and stream beside the building

Nearby Attractions: The Alton Mill is a few minutes away.

Peterborough County

Fowld's Mill

Type: Gristmill
Location: Hastings, Trent River, Peterborough County
When Built: 1871
Current Use: Private Residence
Access: Exterior views only

GPS Location: N 44° 18.631' W 77° 57.294'
Directions: Located on Front St. in the town of Hastings

History: Built in 1871 by James Fowlds, it operated as a gristmill. It was converted to a hydroelectric plant in 1912, and later to a private residence.

Photography Tips: At the right side of the mill property there is a small parking area, and you can set up for photographs from the back near the river without trespassing on mill property.

Nearby Attractions:
King's Mill and O'Hara Mill are a short drive away.

Hope Sawmill

Type: Sawmill
Location: Keene, Indian River, Peterborough County
When Built: 1836
Current Use: Museum exhibit
Access: Public access

GPS Location: N 44° 17.280 ' W 78° 10.260'
Directions: From the town of Keene, go north on County Rd. 34 for 3.5 km. and turn right on Lang Rd.. After 1.8 km., turn left on Hope Mill Rd. and it is a short distance to the entrance.

History: Built in 1836 on the Indian River, it operated as a sawmill and later a carding mill. It is still on the original site and is open to the public as a museum exhibit.

Photography Tips:Excellent spots to set up, and you can include the dam easily.

Nearby Attractions: Lang Mill is a short drive.

Lang Mill

Type: Gristmill
Location: Lang, Indian River, Peterborough County
When Built: 1846
Current Use: Exhibit
Access: Public Access

GPS Location: N 44° 16.572' W 78° 10.278'
Directions: Located at the Lang Conservation Area on North Lang Rd. in the village of Lang

History: Built in 1846 by Thomas Short, it was later operated by William Lang about 1872. It continued operation until 1965, when it was bought by the Otonabee Region Conservation Authority.

Photography Tips: A great looking mill, the river and dam provide some wonderful wide shots.

Nearby Attractions: The Hope Sawmill is a few minutes away

Needler's Mill

Type: Sawmill and Flourmill
Location: Millbrook, Baxter Creek, Peterborough County
When Built: Moved here in 1909
Current Use: Exhibit in Conservation Area
Access: Public access

GPS Location: N 44° 8.963' W 78° 26.868'
Directions: In the town of Millbrook turn south from King St. (County Rd. 21) on Needler's Lane and the mill is a short distance at the end.

History: This is the third mill on this site, having been moved here in 1909 from Cedar Valley after a fire destroyed it's predecessor and it was in operation until 1974. It is currently unoccupied after local citizens saved it from demolition in 1982

Photography Tips: Good exterior vies available from the front and sides.

Nearby Attractions: The Hope Sawmill and Lang Mill are about 40 minutes drive.

York County

Bruce's Gristmill

Type: Gristmill
Location: Whitchurch-Stouffville, Rouge River, York County
When Built: 1858
Current Use: Exhibit
Access: Good exterior views and occasionally open to interior

GPS Location: N 43° 56.964' W 79° 20.736'
Directions: Located in Bruce Mills Conservation Area at 3291 Stouffville Road (Regional Rd. 14) in Whitchurch-Stouffville.

History: Built in 1858 and powered by an overshot water wheel, it is one of Ontario's oldest gristmills. It operated until the 1960s and has since been fully restored.

Photography Tips: Good exterior views from all sides. In the right seasons, look for wildflowers to use in the foreground

Nearby Attractions: Roblin's Mill is about a half hour drive.

Gooderham and Worts Distillery

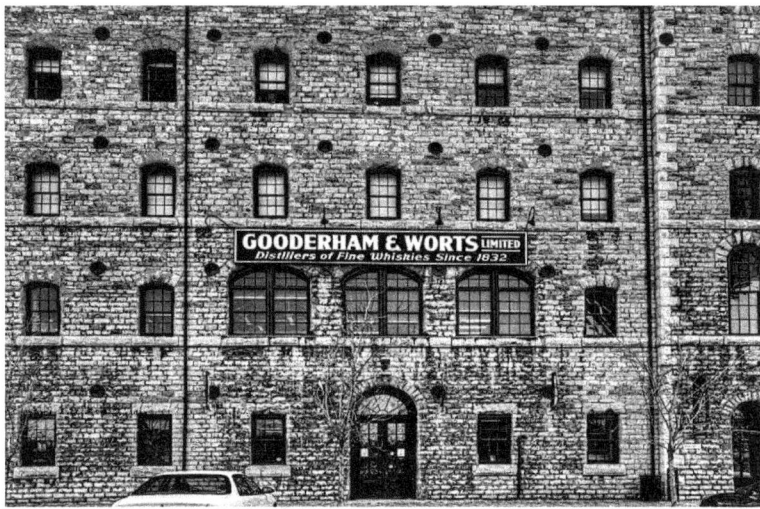

Type: Gristmill and distillery
Location: Toronto, York County
When Built: 1859
Current Use: Commercial
Access: Great exterior views

GPS Location: N 43° 39.042' W 79° 21.582'
Directions: Located on Mill Street in the distillery district in Toronto.

History: James Worts and William Gooderham partnered to build a milling operation in 1831. In 1832 Wort's wife dies during childbirth and the distraught husband killed himself. Gooderham continues the business in partnership with Wort's oldest son, James. The business expands to include a distillery and many other buildings. The present five story stone mill is built in 1859. The area has been renovated to hold commercial business and is a major sight for film work.

Photography Tips: The complex of thirty Victorian buildings offers plenty of scope for great images.

Nearby Attractions: The distillery area as a whole is worth investing some time in.

Markham Cider Mill

Type: Cider Mill
Location: Markham, York County
When Built: Ca. 1880 for earliest portions
Current Use: Exhibit
Access: Exterior views and occasional interior

GPS Location: N 43° 53.661' W 79° 15.877'
Directions: Found at 9350 Markham St. (Highway 48) just north of 16th St. in Markham

History: The mill and its equipment is made up from parts of three older mills. It was re-built on the present site and opened for viewing in 1983

Photography Tips: There are usually nice elements like flowers and an apple tree that can be used in the foreground. At times, the interior equipment is open and can be photographed

York County

Nearby Attractions:
The grounds of the Markham Heritage Village are very interesting including a Saw Mill

Markham Saw Mill

Type: Saw Mill
Location: Markham, York County
When Built: 1851 (Re-built 1982)
Current Use: Exhibit
Access: Exterior views and occasional interior

GPS Location: N 43° 53.661' W 79° 15.877'
Directions: Found at 9350 Markham St. (Highway 48) just north of 16th St. in Markham

History: The original saw mill was built and operated by the Ratcliffe family in 1851. It was located on the Little Rouge River and was water powered until 1936 when diesel power was used. It ceased operations in 1936 and was moved to the museum in the 1970s. After a 1982 fire, it was re-built using materials from an old barn.

Photography Tips: There are usually nice elements like flowers that can be used in the foreground.

Nearby Attractions: The grounds of the Markham Heritage Village are very interesting including a Cider Mill

Old Mill at Toronto

Type: Gristmill
Location: Toronto, Humber River, York County
When Built: 1914
Current Use: Restaurant
Access: Exterior views

GPS Location: N 43° 39.068' W 79° 29.998'

Directions: Found at 45 Old Mill Road in Toronto

History: The present building replaced a seven story gristmill built in 1848 which was destroyed by a fire.

Photography Tips: The middle courtyard of the mill offers some great wide views

Nearby Attractions: The Gooderham and Worts Distillery District is a short drive

Roblin's Mill

Type: Gristmill
Location: Toronto, Millpond, York County
When Built: 1842
Current Use: Exhibit
Access: Good interior and exterior views

GPS Location: N 43° 46.353' W 79° 30.930'
Directions: Found just north of Highway 401 at 1000 Murray Ross Parkway in Toronto.

History: Built in Ameliasburg in 1842 by Owen Roblin, it operated as a gristmill until 1920. In 1960 it was dismantled and re-built at Black Creek Pioneer Village in Toronto.

Photography Tips: You need to carefully pick your spot along the fence line to avoid obstructing trees. The interior offers details of an operational water powered gristmill.

Nearby Attractions: The whole of Black Creek Pioneer Village is worth spending time at, but look for the Snider Cider Mill as well.

Schomberg Feed mill

Type: Feed Mill
Location: Schomberg, York County
When Built: 1884
Current Use: Commercial
Access: Exterior Views
GPS Location: N 44° 00.279' W 79° 41.057'

Directions: Located on Main St. in Schomberg at the corner of Highway 9 and 27

History: Built in 1884 by Anderson Tegart, it operated until 1927 when the lower cost of trucking straight to market became more advantageous. Its peak was around 1900 when the railway was built nearby.

Photography Tips: There are nice wide views available and a bit of detail as well.

Nearby Attractions: The Nicolston Gristmill is only a short drive.

Snider's Cider Mill

Type: Cider Mill
Location: Toronto, York County
When Built: 1840
Current Use: Exhibit
Access: Good interior and exterior views

GPS Location: N 43° 46.353' W 79° 30.930'

Directions: Found just north of Highway 401 at 1000 Murray Ross Parkway in Toronto.

History: Built in North York in 1940. In 1960 it was dismantled and re-built at Black Creek Pioneer Village in Toronto.

Photography Tips: Good interior view of the press but you may need a tripod

Nearby Attractions: The whole of Black Creek Pioneer Village is worth spending time at, but look for the Roblin's Mill as well.

Stiver Mill

Type: Feed Mill
Location: Unionville, York County
When Built: 1916
Current Use: Abandoned
Access: Good exterior views

GPS Location: N 43° 51.856' W 79° 18.714'
Directions: Located on Station Lane in Unionville (Markham)

History: Built by Charles and Francis Stiver in 1916 to replace a Matthew Grain Company structure which had been damaged by fire. It was in operation until 1968. In 1993 the property was purchased by the town of Markham. One of the descendents of the original owners is looking at uses to save the structure.

Photography Tips: Long views of the mill can include the railway tracks. You need to pick your spot carefully to lessen obstructions.

Nearby Attractions: Bruce's Mill and Roblin's Mill are a short drive.

Todmorden Mills

Type: Paper Mill
Location: Toronto, Don River, York County
When Built: 1825
Current Use: Museum
Access: Public access

GPS Location: N 43° 41.208' W 79° 21.618'

Directions: The mill is located on Todmorden Mills Rd., off Pottery Rd by the Don Mills Parkway in Toronto. Access from the Don Valley Parkway is being changed. Check the current entrance on the Mill website below.

History: The area was developed by Aaron and Isaiah Skinner who received a land grant from the Lieutenant-Governor of Upper Canada, John Simcoe. It was given for the purpose of their building of a lumber mill to supply needed building materials to the growing area. The present brick building dates from 1825.

Photography Tips: You can use a wide range of lens, close up for details or more distant landscapes.

Nearby Attractions: The Old Mill at Toronto is about 30 minutes away.

Eastern Ontario Region

Frontenac County

Babcock Mill

Type: Sawmill
Location: Odessa, Millhaven Creek, Frontenac County
When Built: 1856
Current Use: Museum
Access: Public access

GPS Location: N 44° 16.336' W 76° 43.147'
Directions: From Highway 401 west of Kingston, take exit 599 south on County Rd. 6. After 300 m., turn right on Mud Lake Rd. South, and then right on Main St. After a left on Bridge St., the mill is about 500 m.

History: Built in 1856, it has been used as a sawmill, planning mill and box factory. It discontinued operations in 1994 and is now a museum.

Photography Tips: There are easy and excellent views, especially across from the creek.

Nearby Attractions: The Newburgh Mill is nearby.

Bedford Mill

Type: Gristmill
Location: Bedford Mills, Bedford Mills Falls, Frontenac County
When Built: 1848
Current Use: Workshop of a private house
Access: Privately owned but easily seen and photographed

GPS Location: N 44° 36.241' W 76° 24.346'
Directions:
From the Town of Salem, go northeast on County Rd. 12 and turn right on Conc. 9. and continue on Perth Rd. (Regional Rd 10). You will see signs for Bedford Mills after 5.6 km.

History: Although Bedford Mills is now considered a ghost town, it was once a thriving industrial centre.
The area was developed by Benjamin Tett, who had immigrated to Canada in 1820. He bought the land in anticipation of the building of the Rideau Canal and leases a portion to the Chaffey brothers

who build the first mill in 1832. They also built the mill at Chaffey's Lock. Tett purchased it from them and the present mill was built in 1848.
The mill closed in 1916 after it became non-competitive due to lack of resources and the Rideau Canal declined due to the pressure of the Railways. It is still a popular destination for a family outing.

Photography Tips: Opportunities for great images are numerous. As well as the mill, there is the powerhouse and the waterfalls.

Nearby Attractions: Chaffey's Lock Mill is nearby.

Bell Rock Mill

Type: Gristmill
Location: Bellrock, Frontenac County
When Built: Not known
Current Use: Abandoned
Access: Private and posted, good exterior views

GPS Location: N 44° 28.562' W 76° 45.742'
Directions: Found near the east end of Mill Street in Bell Rock

History: I have no historic information on this mill

Photography Tips: The private property makes this a difficult mill to photograph. The owner of the property across from the mill gave me permission to take this image from the bottom of his garden.

Nearby Attractions: Petworth Mill Ruins is only a few minutes drive from here.

Chaffey's Lock Mill

Type: Grist Mill
Location: Chaffey's Lock, Rideau Canal, Frontenac County
When Built: 1872
Current Use: Private residence
Access: Private but the exterior is easily seen and photographed.

GPS Location: N 44° 34.755' W 76° 19.249'
Directions: From Highway 15 northwest of Elgin, take Chaffey's Lock Rd. (County Rd 9) for about 9 km. till you reach Chaffey's Lock on the Rideau Canal

Frontenac County

History: The first mill at this site was built by brothers Samuel and Benjamin Chaffey in 1822. Samuel Chaffey died of malaria in 1827 as it was rampant in that mosquito infested area of Canada. A large number of the laborers who built the Rideau Canal also perished from it. It was demolished when the Rideau Canal and Chaffey's Lock was built.
The present mill was built in 1872 by John Chaffey, Samuel's nephew. It is presently a private residence.

Photography Tips: Although the building is private, there are many public areas of the lock where you can see and photograph it.

Nearby Attractions: The Lock and the Lockmaster's House offer additional items of interest.

Jackson's Mill (Glen Coe Mill)

Type: Gristmill
Location: Kingston, Collins Creek, Frontenac County
When Built: About 1850
Current Use: Private Residence
Access: Exterior only

GPS Location: N 44° 17.806' W 76° 33.598'
Directions: From Highway 401, take Exit 611 north, on County Rd. 38 and take the first right on McIvor Rd., and then left on Jackson Mill Rd. The mill is at the end of the road on the left.

History: Built as a Gristmill about 1850 and operated as such until about 1900, at which time it saw use as a sawmill. In 1961 it was sold and renovated as a private residence.

Photography Tips: The mill is on private property and the only good view is from the road north of the property.

Nearby Attractions: The Kingston Woolen Mill is a short drive away.

Kingston Woolen Mill

Type: Woolen Mill
Location: Kingston, Cataraqui River, Frontenac County
When Built: 1881
Current Use: Commercial companies
Access: Exterior access

Frontenac County

GPS Location: N 44° 14.538' W 76° 28.800'
Directions: Located at 2 Cataraqui St. in Kingston.

History: Built in Kingston in 1881, it had a large additional portion added in 1889.

Photography Tips: This is a huge structure so you need a wide lens, or concentrate on details.

Nearby Attractions: Jackson's Mill is a short drive.

Lower Brewers Mill (Washburn Mill)

Type: Gristmill
Location: Brewers Mills, Cataraqui River, Frontenac County
When Built: 1861
Current Use: Artist's Studio
Access: Outside easily seen and photographed

GPS Location: N 44° 23.341' W 76° 19.465'
Directions: From the Village of Washburn on Highway 15, take Washburn Rd. north, the mill and the lock are less than 1 km.

History: There has been a mill at this site before the Rideau Canal was in the later part of the 1820's but it was purchased a destroyed during the building of the canal. The present mill was built in 1861 as a gristmill. It is presently used as an artist's studio.

Photography Tips: There are multiple points to photograph from, directly across the water course being one of the best.

Nearby Attractions: Chaffey's Lock Mill is a reasonable driving distance.

Petworth Mill Ruins

Type: Probably a Gristmill
Location: Petworth, Napanee River, Frontenac County
When Built: About 1840
Current Use: Ruins
Access: Posted, exterior views only

GPS Location: N 44° 25.024' W 76° 45.430'
Directions: In the small settlement of Petworth, the remains of the mill are beside the bridge over the Napanee River.

History: The remains of a mill found by the river is one of several mills which were built by Stephenson and Lott in the 1840s. The thriving town had some excitement in the 1870's when farmers from nearby Verona blew up the Petworth dam after being upset by flooded fields and crops.

Photography Tips: There are good exterior views by the gate and from the bridge.

Nearby Attractions: The Bellrock Mill is only a few minutes drive

Frontenac County

Lanark County

Boulton Brown Mill

Type: Grist Mill
Location: Carleton Place, Mississippi River, Lanark County
When Built: 1869 with additions in 1885
Current Use: Condominiums
Access: Private but the exterior is easy to see and photograph

GPS Location: N 45° 08.458' W 76° 08.728'
Directions:
Located on Mill St. near the intersection of Beckwith St. in Carleton Place.

History:
The site has been used as a milling business since the 1820's with the present building dating from 1869. In 1970 a fire ended the milling business and it stood vacant over 10 years until it was developed as a condominium.

Photography Tips: The only reasonable places to set up off of private property is on the street in front, although there may be a telephoto angle available from across the river.

Nearby Attractions: The Gillie's Mill and McArthur Mill are a short walk from this one.

Code's Mill

Type: Mill Type
Location: Perth, Tay River, Lanark County
When Built: 1842 (Tannery) became a Knitting Mill in 1884
Current Use: Restaurant and stores
Access: Open to the public

GPS Location: N 44° 53.992' W 76° 15.111'
Directions: Found at the intersection of Wilson St. W., and Herriott St. in Perth.

History: The building was constructed in 1842 for use as a tannery. T. Ode purchased it in 1882 and converted it to a knitting mill.

Additions were added in 1894 and 1903. The mill ceased operations in 1959 and the building is presently used by a variety of stores including a restaurant.

Photography Tips: There are easy places to set up for a wide view of the building.

Nearby Attractions: There is a park across the road with an interesting bridge and a small waterfall.

Collie Mill Ruins

Type: Woolen Mill
Location: Appleton, Mississippi River, Lanark County
When Built: 1862?
Current Use: Ruins
Access: Visible from the other side of the Mississippi River. No access as it is fenced and posted

GPS Location: N 45° 10.982' W 76° 07.491'

Directions: Found on Old Mill Lane in Appleton, Ontario. The remaining ruins may well be removed in the future,

History: The mills recent history has been interesting. After the mill was destroyed by fire in 2007, the owner, Mr. Dulmage pleaded guilty to environmental charges. Mr. Dulmage was formerly the mayor of Carleton Place.
Its past history is not as easy to find but it may have been built in 1862.

Photography Tips: The only reasonable place to photograph the ruins is from the other side of the Mississippi River, across the Appleton Rapids. I used a 200 mm lens.

Nearby Attractions: The mills at Carleton Place are nearby.

Gillies Mill

Type: Woolen Mill
Location: Carleton Place, Mississippi River, Lanark County
When Built: 1875
Current Use: Commercial

Access: private but easy views of exterior

GPS Location: N 45° 08.458' W 76° 08.728'
Directions: On Mill St. in Carleton by the bridge which crosses the Mississippi River.

History: Built in 1875 for the purpose of Machine Works by John Gillies and F. Beyer, it was purchased by Bates and Innes and converted to millwork.

Photography Tips: While the building is private, there are excellent vantage point which incorporate the river in the foreground.

Nearby Attractions: Boulton Brown Mill and McArthur Mill are a short walk.

Maberly Sawmill

Type: Sawmill
Location: Maberly, Lanark County
When Built: Not known
Current Use: Abandoned

Lanark County

Access: Private

GPS Location: N 44° 50.221' W 76° 32.381'
Directions: On Elphin Maberly Rd. in the Village of Maberly

History: Not known

Photography Tips: A front view from the road is all that is available as both sides are obstructed.

Nearby Attractions: Adam's Mill and Bowes Mill are nearby

Maple Leaf Mill

Type: Flourmill
Location: Almonte, Mississippi River, Lanark County
When Built: Ca. 1870
Current Use: May be renovated for condominiums
Access: Private but excellent exterior views
GPS Location: N 45° 13.517' W 76° 11.852'
Directions:

On Main St. E. by the railway track in Almonte. Better views are available from the river walk on the other side of the river.

History: One of four mills that have survived in Almonte, of the many that were operated at one time, taking advantage of the power supplied by the Mississippi River,

Photography Tips: There are good views from the river walk across from the mill, including using the railway bridge in the foreground.

Nearby Attractions: Rosamund Mill, Victoria Woolen Mill, Maple Leaf Mill and Thoburn Mill are all a short walk.

McArthur Mill

Type: Woolen Mill
Location: Carleton Place, Mississippi River, Lanark County
When Built: 1871
Current Use: Electrical firm
Access: Private but easy view and photographs of exterior available.
GPS Location: N 45° 08.458' W 76° 08.728'

Lanark County

Directions: By the corner of Princess and Mill Streets in Carleton Place.

History: This five story stone structure was built in 1871 by Archibald McArthur as a woolen Mill. He manufactured fine worsteds and tweeds. It was later purchased by Bates and Innes who made blankets and cloths.

Photography Tips: Easy set up on the bank beside the building on public property. Note the waterwheel machinery on the side of the building.

Nearby Attractions: The Gillie's Mill and Boulton Brown Mill are a short walk from this one.

Merrickville Ruins

Type: Ruins of multiple mills
Location: Merrickville, Rideau River, Lanark County
When Built: About 1860
Current Use: Ruins
Access: Public access

GPS Location: N 44° 55.102' W 75° 50.732'
Directions: Found on West Broadway St. in the town of Merrickville

History: This complex of ruins beside the Rideau canal includes the remains of five mills all dated to about 1860.

Photography Tips: You can wander freely among the ruins. A wide angle lens will prove useful.

Nearby Attractions: The Spencerville Mill is a short drive.

Mill of Kintail

Type: Gristmill
Location: Almonte, Indian River, Lanark County
When Built: 1830
Current Use: Part of the Mill of Kintail Conservation Area
Access: Grounds are open dawn to dusk.

GPS Location: N 45° 14.646' W 76° 15.503'

Directions: From the Town of Almonte, take County Rd 49 to Regional Rd., 29 and go right. After 4 km, turn left on Clayton Rd. Go 1.5 km on Clayton and go right on Ramsay Concession. The entrance to the Mill of Kintail Conservation Area is about 2 km.

History: Built in 1830 by a Scottish immigrant named John Baird. In 1930, it was restored by the sculptor, Robert Tait McKenzie and subsequently became part of the Mill of Kintail Conservation Area.

Photography Tips: There are excellent views from the bridge looking along the Indian River to the mill.

Nearby Attractions: The trails of the Conservation area are worthwhile.

Rosamond Mill

Type: Woolen Mill
Location: Almonte, Mississippi River, Lanark County
When Built: 1866
Current Use: Condominium
Access: Private but easy exterior views

Lanark County

GPS Location: N 45° 13.648' W 76° 11.991'
Directions: From the Town of Carleton Place, take Mary St., off of Main St. E (Highway 49) and drive to the end.

History: The Rosamond Mill was built in 1866 and added to in subsequent years. It was a large woolen operation that was recognized worldwide as an innovative operation and it continued operations until the 1980's when it closed due to factors like the increasing use of synthetics. At one point it operated 90 looms.

Photography Tips:
Easy to photograph from the street or the parking lot.

Nearby Attractions: Victoria Woolen Mill, Maple Leaf Mill, and Thoburn Mill are all within walking distance. The Mississippi Valley Textile Museum is beside the Rosamond Mill.

Thoburn Mill

Type: Woolen Mill
Location: Almonte, Mississippi River, Lanark County
When Built: 1918
Current Use: Condominiums
Access: Private but there are easy exterior views.

GPS Location: N 45° 13.517' W 76° 11.852'
Directions: In Almonte, go east on Mill St. off of Main St E (Highway 49). Left on Little Bridge Road takes you to the mill at 83 Little Bridge St.

History: The mill was owned and built by William Thoburn to replace a mill destroyed in a fire in 1918. The original mill, the Brown Mill was built in about 1820. The Thoburn Mill currently houses condominiums.

Photography Tips: The best spot for an exterior shot is from the side of the rail track behind it.

Nearby Attractions: The Rosamond Mill, Victoria Woolen Mill, and Maple Leaf Mill are in walking distance.

Victoria Woolen Mill (Rosamond Mill 1)

Type: Woolen Mill
Location: Almonte, Mississippi River, Lanark County
When Built: 1857
Current Use: Condominium and commercial
Access: Private but exterior easily viewed

GPS Location: N 45° 13.517' W 76° 11.852'
Directions: On the corner of Main St. W. (Highway 49), and Mill St. in Almonte

History: Built in 1857 by James Rosamond. It was built on the same site as Almonte's first woolen mill, the Ramsay Mill which burned in 1852. You need only look at the waterfall beside the building to understand why it was a preferred site, as it provided the water power to run the mill.
If you take a close look at the building, you will see that the top two floors are constructed from a lighter stone. This is because it is an addition to the original building.

Photography Tips: Don't neglect the waterfall behind the building as it can be spectacular when there is a lot of water in the system.

Nearby Attractions:
The Rosamond Mill, Maple Leaf Mill and Thoburn Mill are nearby.

Wood's Mill

Type: Grain Mill
Location: Smith's Falls, Rideau River, Lanark County
When Built: 1852
Current Use: Parks Canada
Access: Exterior only at present

GPS Location: N 44° 53.821' W 76° 01.266'
Directions: Found at 34 Beckwith St. S. in Smith's Falls.

History: There are three structures in the complex, the west mill, a grain mill built in 1852, the east mill, a grain mill built in 1890, and a grain elevator, also built in 1890.

They were purchased by Parks Canada because they were historically important as an early industrial complex.

Photography Tips: Easy to take multiple angle shots of the exterior.

Nearby Attractions: Code's Mill in Perth is about a half hour drive away.

Leeds and Grenville County

Delta Mill (Old Stone Mill)

Type: Gristmill
Location: Delta, Leeds and Grenville County
When Built: 1810
Current Use: Museum
Access: Public Access

GPS Location: N 44° 36.577' W 76° 07.345'
Directions: Located in the village of Delta on County Rd. 42.

History: William Jones built this beautiful stone mill in the village of Delta in 1810, and it is one of the oldest grist mills that has survived.

In 1963 it came into the hands of the newly formed Delta Mill Society, a non-profit Corporation dedicated to its maintenance and continuation. It has been designated by Canada as a

National Historic Site, and by Ontario under the Ontario Heritage Act.

Photography Tips: This is a premier destination for photographers. The pond beside it offers great opportunities for reflections and there are plenty of details for interesting close ups.

Nearby Attractions: It is about 40 minutes drive to the Chaffey Lock Mill.

Island City Mill

Type: Flour mill
Location: Brockville, Leeds and Grenville County
When Built: 1905 became a mill operation, the building may be older
Current Use: Commercial
Access: Good exterior views

GPS Location: N 44° 35.234' W 75° 41.283'
Directions: In Brockville, go through the alley near 189 King St. W. and you will find the mill in an area know as Sheridan Mews.

History: I have little information on this mill. The mill apparently began milling wheat in 1905 and currently holds commercial businesses.

Photography Tips: There are easy exterior views on all sides.

Nearby Attractions: Shepherd Gristmill is only two blocks away.

Roddick Mill Ruins

Type: Gristmill?
Location: Lyndhurst, Leeds and Grenville County
When Built: Probably about 1810
Current Use: Ruins
Access: Private, ask permission

GPS Location: N 44° 32.987' W 76° 07.516'
Directions: Found on 2nd Rd , south of the bridge in Lyndhurst

History: Some of the principles who built the Delta Mill are said to be involved in this operation. An archaeological dig at the site by Queen's University has cast some doubt that it was operated as a mill but may have been a foundry.

Photography Tips: If you receive permission, there is a rough trail at the south end which allows close views of the ruins.

Nearby Attractions:
The Delta Mill is about 20 minutes drive.

Shepherd's Gristmill

Type: Gristmill
Location: Brockville, Buell's Creek, Leeds and Grenville County
When Built: 1852
Current Use: Restaurant
Access: Exterior views

GPS Location: N 44° 35.175' W 75° 41.278'
Directions: Found at 123 Water St. West in Brockville

History: Robert Shepherd bought a sawmill near this site in 1836 and in 1852 he added this gristmill. The sawmill was torn down and the gristmill ceased operation by 1883. It was used as a storage building for many years, and was gutted and renovated as a restaurant beginning in 1982. It was designated under the Ontario Heritage Act in 1980.

Photography Tips: There are excellent exterior views from most sides.

Nearby Attractions: The Island City Mill is only a short walk from here.

Spencerville Mill

Type: Gristmill
Location: Spencerville, South Nation River, Leeds and Grenville County
When Built: 1864
Current Use: Museum Exhibit
Access: Public access
GPS Location: : 44° 50.512' W 75° 32.697'

Directions: Found on Water St. in Spencerville

History: Peleg Spencer built a sawmill on the site in 1812, and in 1864 Robert Fairbaird built a stone building which operated as a gristmill. The operation had various owners and only ceased milling operations in 1972. The property is currently a museum maintained by the Spencerville Mill Foundation.

Photography Tips: There is a variety of excellent views, especially including the dam beside it. Look for details as well.

Nearby Attractions: The Merrickville Ruins are only a short drive from here.

Windmill Lighthouse

Type: Gristmill
Location: Wexford, Leeds and Grenville County
When Built: 1873
Current Use: Historic exhibit
Access: Both interior and exterior views

GPS Location: N 44° 43.254' W 75° 29.220'
Directions: from the village of Wexford, just east of Prescott, take Windmill Rd off King St and you will find it on your right after a short drive.

History: The building began as a windmill and operated as a gristmill until it was converted to a lighthouse in 1873. It is the site of the 1838 Battle of the Windmill, where Canadian rebels and American allies fought with British troops.

Photography Tips: Excellent exterior views. The inside is open daily in July and August and on weekends in June and September.

Nearby Attractions: The three mills at Upper Canada Village, Asselstine's, Beach's and Bellamy's, are about a half hour drive.

Leeds and Grenville County

Lennox and Addington County

Hoopers Mill (Newburgh Mill)

Type: Gristmill
Location: Newburgh, Napanee River, Lennox and Addington County
When Built: ca.1850s?
Current Use: Private
Access: Exterior views

GPS Location: N 44° 19.394' W 76° 52.605'
Directions: Found at 28 Front St. in Newburgh

History: The information I have found indicates this mill may have been built in the 1850s. It has been beautifully renovated as a private residence.

Photography Tips: The grounds are private property but there are a few good views from the road in front.

Nearby Attractions: There are two mill ruins nearby in Newburgh, the Thompson Papermill Ruins and the Union Flourmill Ruins.

Thompson Paper Mill Ruins

Type: Paper Mill
Location: Newburgh, Napanee River, Lennox and Addington County
When Built: 1880
Current Use: Ruins
Access: Private but visible from road

GPS Location: N 44° 19.394' W 76° 52.605'
Directions: Found at the corner of Earl and Elgin St. in Newburgh.

History: Brothers John and James Thompson, and J.W. Rooklidge built the Newburgh Paper Mills in 1880. The mill operated until 1932 when it was dismantled.

Photography Tips: On private property but visible from the road.

Nearby Attractions:
The Hoopers Mill and the Ruins of the Union Flourmill are a short walk from here.

Union Flour Mills Ruins

Type: Flour Mill
Location: Newburgh, Napanee River, Lennox and Addington County
When Built: About 1840
Current Use: Ruins
Access: Public access

GPS Location: N 44° 19.394' W 76° 52.605'
Directions: Found behind a vacant lot beside 28 Front St. in Newburgh

History: Between 1820 and 1860, Newburgh was a thriving community with a large number of mills along the Napanee River. I have no information about the demise of this mill but there was a major fire in 1887 which destroyed 84 buildings and this may have been one of the victims.

Photography Tips: There is not much remaining to photograph.

Nearby Attractions: The Hoopers Mill is nearby, as is the ruins of the Thomson Paper Mill.

Ottawa-Carleton Region

Watson's Mill (The Long Island Mill)

Type: Gristmill
Location: Manotick, Rideau River, Ottawa-Carleton Region
When Built: 1860
Current Use: Museum
Access: Public access

GPS Location: N 45° 13.361' W 75° 41.001'
Directions: Located a 5525 Dickinson in Manotick.

History: Built in 1860 by Moss Dickinson and Joseph Currier and operated as a gristmill. It was in operation until 1972 when it was sold to Rideau Valley Conservation Authority.

Photography Tips:This is a beautiful mill and there are numerous excellent views. In particular, cross the bridge at the dam and you will find a good vantage point downriver.

Nearby Attractions: The Merrickville Ruins are about 40 minutes drive from here.

Perth County

Adam's Mill (Glen Tay Mill)

Type: Originally a Sawmill and then a Gristmill
Location: Glen Tay, Tay River, Perth County
When Built: Prior to 1820
Current Use: Private Residence
Access: Private Property, easy to see and photograph from the road

GPS Location: N 44° 52.597' W 76° 18.230'
Directions: From The Village of Glen Tay on Christie Lake Rd (County Rd 6), go south on Glen Tay Rd for 800m. till you reach the Tay River. From the bridge you can see the mill.

History:Built prior to 1820 by Abraham Parsall, it was purchased by Joshua Adams in that year. In the late Nineteenth Century it operated as a hydroelectric plant. In 1926, the dam gave way and the resulting flood took out the Glen Tay Bridge and flooded parts of Perth. The restored mill is now a private residence.

Photography Tips: The building is on private property but there is an excellent point to set up for photographs near the bridge.

Nearby Attractions: Bowe's and Code's Mill are both nearby.

Prince Edward County

Chisholm Mills

Type: Feed mill and Sawmill
Location: Chisholm Mills, Moira River, Prince Edward County
When Built: 1857 or earlier
Current Use: Empty although the Chisholm Lumber Co. continues to operate next door.
Access: Exterior views only

GPS Location: N 44° 21.205' W 77° 18.475'
Directions: From the town of Roslin, take Shannonville Rd. east for about 2 km. to Chisholm Mills. When Shannonville Rd. goes right (south), you will see the mill at the Moira River bridge.

History: William Chisholm purchased the mill property in 1857 and it has been in the Chisholm family to the present day. The mill building is currently not in use.

Photography Tips: Great views available from across the river below the bridge.

Nearby Attractions: The Latta Mill Ruins and the Lonsdale Mill are a short drive.

Glenora Mill (Van Alstine Mill)

Type: Mill Type
Location: Glenora, Prince Edward County
When Built: 1806
Current Use: Private Residence
Access: Exterior views only

GPS Location: N 44° 02.093' W 77° 03.579'
Directions: In the village of Glenora, the mill is beside the ferry terminal at the end of the Loyalist Parkway.

History: Built in 1806 and owned by Peter Van Alstine, it was operated as a Gristmill. At one point it was leased by Sir John A. Macdonald's father. It is currently a private residence.

Photography Tips: The only place you can set up on public property is between the ferry terminal and the mill.

Nearby Attractions: Scott's Mill is about 20 minutes drive.

Scott's Mill

Type: Lumber mill
Location: Milford, Mill Pond, Prince Edward County
When Built: About 1815
Current Use: Exhibit
Access: Exterior access

GPS Location: N 43° 56.442' W 77° 06.142'
Directions: Found at the corner of Crowes Rd. and Scott Mill Road in the village of Milford.

History:
The building of this mill was the impetus for the settlement of Milford.
The building was purchased by the Prince Edward Region Conservation Authority and is well maintained.

Photography Tips:
Good views from front and sides.

Nearby Attractions:
The Glenora Mill is about 20 minutes drive.

Renfrew County

Balaclava Mill

Type: Sawmill
Location: Balaclava, Constant Creek, Renfrew County
When Built: 1855
Current Use: Abandoned
Access: Posted against entry but easily seen and photographed

GPS Location: N 45° 23.407' W 78° 07.491'
Directions: From Dacre on Highway 132, go northeast on Scotch Bush Rd. to the settlement of Balaclava. The mill is on the east side of the road.

History Built in 1855, it was said to be producing a million board feet of lumber per week in the thriving town of Balaclava. It was closed in 1959 and Balaclava is considered a ghost town. I was there in a driving rain and the waters were flooding. With the building in such poor condition, I thought I might see it swept away. If you want to see it, you may want to plan an early trip.

Photography Tips: Easy to photograph from the road. Lots of texture to it, so consider close ups to bring that out.

Nearby Attractions: The McDougall Mill in Renfrew is a 40 minute drive.

Bowe's Mill (Fraser Mill, Tay View Mill)

Type: Sawmill and Gristmill
Location: Glen Tay, Tay River, Renfrew County
When Built: Early 1820's
Current Use: Museum
Access: Private but visible from the road.

GPS Location: N 44° 51.668' W 76° 18.906'
Directions: From the Village of Glen Tay go west on Christie Lake Rd. (County Rd. 6) and turn south on Bowes Rd. The mill is found after about 1.6 km.

History: Operated from the 1820's, first as a sawmill, and then as a gristmill, it went through a succession of owners before being sold to the Town of Perth in 1895. The town converted it to a hydroelectric generating station which supplied the towns first electrical supply. Anson Bowe's purchased it in 1932 after converting it back to a gristmill which was operated until a 1952 fire. The building was restored by the Bowes family as a museum.

Photography Tips: Good positions can be found from the public road.

Nearby Attractions: Adam's Mill is only a few minutes away

Eganville Gristmill Ruins

Type: Gristmill
Location: Eganville, Bonnecherre River, Renfrew County
When Built: 1849
Current Use: Ruins
Access: Open

GPS Location: N 45° 32.153' W 77° 05.56
Directions: From the Town of Eganville, go south off Bonnecherre Rd E., on Grist Mill Rd for a short while. The ruins are in the river.

History: The Gristmill was built by John Egan, for whom the Town of Eganville is named, in 1849. He died of cholera in 1857. I have no information on the demise of the mill.

Photography Tips: Easy to photograph from the bank of the river.

Nearby Attractions: The McDougall Mill is about 45 minutes drive.

McDougall Mill

Type: Gristmill
Location: Renfrew, Bonnechere River, Renfrew County
When Built: 1855
Current Use: Museum
Access: Open June through September. Their hours available on the link below.

GPS Location: N 45° 28.637' W 76° 41.445'
Directions: The mill is on Arthur Ave, just off Stewart St./Highway 60 in Renfrew. You can also park on the other side of the river on Mutual Ave, and walk over the swinging bridge.

History: The McDougall Mill in Renfrew lies beside the Second Chute on the Bonnechere River in Ontario. It was originally a grist mill built in 1855 by Hudson's Bay Company agent, John Lorne McDougall. In 1969 it became a museum. It is just upstream from a Swinging Bridge built in 1895.

Photography Tips: There are interesting images available incorporating the swinging bridge.

Nearby Attractions: There is a swinging bridge just downstream.

Old Killaloe Mill

Type: Gristmill and Sawmill
Location: Old Killaloe, Old Killaloe Pond, Renfrew County
When Built: 1849 (Rebuilt 1870 after a fire)
Current Use: Private residence
Access: Private but easy views and photographs from the public road

GPS Location: N 45° 32.081' W 77° 24.930'
Directions: From the small Village of Old Killaloe on Highway 512, it is easily seen on the west side of the highway.

History: Originally built in 1849, and after a fire re-built in 1870, the mill was in use until 1930 to grind grain and produced lumber until about 1960.

Photography Tips: There are good open views from the road north of the mill which will include the waterfall. Don't go by the quality of the photo above, which was taken in a raging downpour.

Nearby Attractions: Balaclava Mill is a drive of about an hour.

Renfrew County

Stormont, Dundas and Glengarry County

Asselstine Woolen Mill

Type: Woolen Mill
Location: Morrisburg, Stormont, Dundas and Glengarry County
When Built: 1828
Current Use: Exhibit
Access: Interior and exterior access

GPS Location: N 44° 56.810' W 75° 04.455'
Directions: From Highway 401, take exit 758, and go south on Upper Canada Rd. for 1.7 km and turn left on County Rd. 2. The entrance to Upper Canada Village is 2 km. on the right.

History: The mill was built by Michael Asselstine in 1928 and originally situated near Odessa. It was operational until 1947. It was later moved to Upper Canada Village.

Photography Tips: The outside is rather plain but the inside holds a large amount of operational milling equipment.
To overcome the low light conditions, take along a tripod.

Nearby Attractions: Beach's Sawmill and Bellamy's Mill are also on exhibit at Upper Canada Village

Beach's Sawmill

Type: Sawmill
Location: Morrisburg, Stormont, Dundas and Glengarry County
When Built: 1846
Current Use: Exhibit
Access: Public access

GPS Location: N 44° 56.810' W 75° 04.455'
Directions: From Highway 401, take exit 758, and go south on Upper Canada Rd. for 1.7 km and turn left on County Rd. 2. The entrance to Upper Canada Village is 2 km. on the right.
History: Built by William and Alvin Beach in 1846 and originally located in Heckston, it was operational for many years. It was moved to become an exhibit at Upper Canada Village.

Photography Tips: It can be photographed from all sides and there are nice reflections from the quiet pond.

Nearby Attractions: Asselstine Woolen Mill and Bellamy's Mill are also on exhibit at Upper Canada Village

Bellamy's Mill

Type: Flour mill
Location: Morrisburg, Stormont, Dundas and Glengarry County
When Built: 1822
Current Use: Exhibit
Access: Interior and exterior access

GPS Location: N 44° 56.810' W 75° 04.455'
Directions: From Highway 401, take exit 758, and go south on Upper Canada Rd. for 1.7 km and turn left on County Rd. 2. The entrance to Upper Canada Village is 2 km. on the right.

History: Built by brothers Samuel, Chauncey and Hiram Bellamy in 1822, it was initially located in North Augusta. It was adapted to run by steam power as well as water and is still capable of steam functioning now that it is an exhibit at Upper Canada Village.

Photography Tips: As well as excellent vantage points for the exterior of this stone building, there are interesting items inside. A tripod would be useful for the interior.

Nearby Attractions: Asselstine Woolen Mill and Beach's Sawmill are also on exhibit at Upper Canada Village.

Martintown Mill

Type: Gristmill
Location: Martintown, Aux Raisin River, Stormont, Dundas and Glengarry County
When Built: 1846
Current Use: Museum
Access: Easy exterior views and occasional public interior access

GPS Location: N 45° 09.224' W74° 42.692'
Directions: Located at the south side of Dundas St. in the town of Martintown.

History: Built in 1846 by Alexander McMartin, it operated as gristmill until 1947. It fell into disrepair but has been owned and maintained by the non-profit Martintown Mill Preservation Society since 1997.

Photography Tips: There are excellent exterior views, especially the interesting window layout at the back and as view from across the river.

Nearby Attractions: Priest's Mill is about 45 minutes drive.

Priest's Mill

Type: Gristmill
Location: Alexandria, Mill Pond, Stormont, Dundas and Glengarry County
When Built: 1819
Current Use: Restaurant (Currently closed)
Access: Good exterior views

GPS Location: N 45° 18.604' W 74° 38.137'
Directions: Found on Mills St. South (Highway 34) in Alexandria

History: This stone building was built in 1819 by Father Alexander MacDonnell and came to be known as the Priest's Mill. Alexander MacDonnell later became the first Roman Catholic Bishop of Upper

Canada. The mill operated as a gristmill. It has recently housed a restaurant but this was closed (2011)

Photography Tips: Best positions seem to be from the parking lot beside the mill although there may be cars in your frame.

Nearby Attractions: The nearest mill is the Martintown Mill

Northern Ontario Region

Manitoulin County

Manitowaning Roller Mills

Type: Grist Mill
Location: Manitowaning, Manitoulin County
When Built: 1883
Current Use: Exhibit
Access: Open July and August

GPS Location: N 45° 44.694' W 81° 48.318'
Directions: Found at the waterfront in Manitowaning.

History: Built as a Gristmill and Flour Mill in Manitowaning in 1883. It is now home to an agricultural exhibit which is open daily in July and August.

Photography Tips: If you take a wide view from the hill behind you can include the ship "SS Norisle" at the berth beside it.

Nearby Attractions: The Domtar Paper Mill in Espanola is about an hours drive.

Parry Sound Region

South River Grist Mill

Type: Gristmill
Location: South River, South River, Parry Sound County
When Built: Ca 1890
Current Use: Abandoned
Access: Exterior only

GPS Location: N 45° 50.882' W 79° 22.515'
Directions: from Highway 11 in South River, take Marie St east and go north on Mill Rd. to the bridge over the South River. The mill is to the left.

History: Built in the late 19th century by a man named Downey and operated as a gristmill.

Photography Tips: The clearest view would seem to be from across the river just below the bridge.

Nearby Attractions:
There are no nearby mills.

Simcoe County

Baldwin Mill

Type: Gristmill
Location: Baldwin, Black River, Simcoe County
When Built: 1883
Current Use: Private residence
Access: Exterior views only

GPS Location: N 44° 15.704' W 79° 20.671'
Directions: From the village of Baldwin, the mill can be viewed from the road, Highway 48.

History: This is the third mill on the site, after the first two burned down. It was brought piece by piece from Keswick and completed in 1883. It is now a private residence.

Photography Tips: The mill is on private property but there are views from the highway.

Nearby Attractions: The Sutton Mill and Udora Mill are a short drive.

Bell Gristmill

Type: Gristmill
Location: Utopia, Nottawasaga River, Simcoe County
When Built: 1904
Current Use: Abandoned
Access: Easy exterior views

GPS Location: N 44° 19.695' W 79° 50.072'
Directions: In the town of Utopia, found on Old Mill Rd., just off of Sixth Line

History: Built in 1904 by Richard Bell with the help of his two brothers, Manuel and John. It replaced a mill built in 1860 that burned in 1903. The mill ran on water power until Hurricane Hazel washed out the dam in 1954, and it continued in operation using diesel power until 1965. At that time the owner, Harold Bell, donated the site to the Nottawasaga Valley Conservation Area.

Photography Tips: The exterior has a lot of character and is easily framed from three sides. The wall siding is made of small squares of sheet metal.

Nearby Attractions: The Hillsdale Mill is less than a 30 minute drive.

Coldwater Mill

Type: Gristmill
Location: Coldwater, Coldwater River, Simcoe County
When Built: 1833
Current Use: Restaurant
Access: Easy exterior views

GPS Location: N 44° 42.490' W 79° 38.614'
Directions: Found at 1 Mill Street in Coldwater

History:
Financed by the Ojibwa Indian Tribe, this mill was built in Coldwater in 1833 by Stephen Chapman and Jacob Gill. It was sold to George Copeland in 1849 and operated for over 125 years.

Photography Tips: There are exterior views from many sides. Good clear images available from the parking lot and bridge.

Nearby Attractions: The Marchmont Mill is only a short distance.

Collingwood Gristmill

Type: Gristmill
Location: Collingwood, Simcoe County
When Built: Ca. 1900
Current Use: Exhibit
Access: Good exterior views

GPS Location: N 44° 29.249' W 80° 15.271'
Directions: Found at 879 6th St. In Collingwood

History: Originally built about 1900 and operated as a gristmill. It was run on a Leighley Flywheel engine on diesel and farmers would bring their wheat to it. It was last owned by Bill Akers and moved to the present site at Bygone Days in 1974.

Photography Tips: Easy exterior views and sometimes interior views of the remaining machinery.

Nearby Attractions: The Collingwood Sawmill is on the same site.

Collingwood Saw Mill

Type: Saw Mill
Location: Collingwood, Simcoe County
When Built: Ca. 1900
Current Use: Exhibit
Access: Good exterior views

GPS Location: N 44° 29.249' W 80° 15.271'
Directions: Found at 879 6th St. In Collingwood

History: This building is typical of many small saw mills that could be found in the are around 1900.

Photography Tips: Easy exterior views and sometimes interior views of the remaining machinery.

Nearby Attractions:
The Collingwood Gristmill is on the same site.

Hillsdale Mill

Type: Gristmill
Location: Hillsdale, Sturgeon River, Simcoe County
When Built: 1833
Current Use: Abandoned
Access: Exterior views

GPS Location: N 44° 35.143' W 79° 44.121'
Directions: Located at 1 Mill St. in Hillsdale.

History: Built in 1833 by Thomas Anderson and Jacob Gill for the Ojibway First Nation. The mill was purchased by the Rumble Family in 1907 who operated it for many years. All operations ceased in 1995.

Photography Tips: This is a beautiful weathered building. You will want a variety of lens to get detail and a broad view.

Nearby Attractions:
The Coldwater Mill and Marchmont Mill are a short drive.

Marchmont Mill

Type: Gristmill
Location: Marchmont, Mill pond, Simcoe County
When Built: Ca. 1850
Current Use: Private
Access: Exterior views

GPS Location: N 44° 37.966' W 79° 30.587'
Directions: Found in the Town of Marchmont, on Marchmont Rd. near Hume St.

History: Built from local materials around 1850, it operated until the 1990s. It is now a private residence.

Photography Tips: Good views from the bridge.

Nearby Attractions: The Coldwater Mill is only a few minutes drive.

Nicolston Gristmill

Type: Gristmill
Location: Alliston, Nottawasaga River, Simcoe County
When Built: 1907
Current Use: Commercial
Access: Interior with permission, and good exterior views

GPS Location: N 44° 10.093' W 79° 48.701'
Directions: Located at 5140 5th Line, Alliston, Ontario

History: The original mill on this site, built in 1858, burnt in 1900. It was replaced in 1907 by the present building. The dam burst in 1890 but was re-built and it was latter breached by Hurricane Hazel in 1954.

Photography Tips: There are artifacts as well as flowers which can be used for foreground elements.

Nearby Attractions: The Bell Gristmill is about a half hour drive.

Sutton Mill

Type: Gristmill
Location: Sutton, Black River, Simcoe County
When Built: 1820
Current Use: Commercial
Access: Good exterior views

GPS Location: N 44° 18.294' W 79° 21.654'
Directions: Located at 141 High St. in Sutton West

History:
The first mill on this site was built by the Bourchier brothers, Empire Loyalists who had been given a land grant in 1816. The mill was completed in 1820 and operated until the late 1950s.

It is currently used for commercial purposes.

Photography Tips: There is a great view which includes the Black River in the foreground from the bridge.

Nearby Attractions: The Baldwin Mill and Udora Mill are a short drive.

Udora Mill (Peers Grist Mill)

Type: Gristmill
Location: Udora, Uxbridge River, Simcoe County
When Built: Ca. 1870
Current Use: Abandoned
Access: Exterior only

GPS Location: N 44° 15.648' W 79° 10.650'
Directions: Found on Mill Pond Road, off of Highway 32 in Udora

History:
Built by Thomas and Lancelot Bolster around the 1860s, it operated as a gristmill until it closed in 1975, Its alternate name, Peers Grist Mill, refers to its 90 year ownership by the peers family.

Photography Tips:
There are some great open views from across the river. Close up details and artifacts are available as well.

Nearby Attractions:
Sutton Mill and Baldwin Mill are nearby.

Washago Grist Mill

Type: Gristmill
Location: Washago, Severn River, Simcoe County
When Built: 1873
Current Use: Private residence
Access: Exterior views only

GPS Location: N 44° 45.001'W 79° 19.812'
Directions: Found just off the main street in Washago.

History:
The mill was built by Abial Marshall in 1873 and operated as a gristmill until 1970. It is currently a private residence.

Photography Tips:
There are some front views which include the mill race.

Nearby Attractions:
The Coldwater Mill and the Marchmont Mill are nearby.

Sudbury Region

Domtar Paper Mill

Type: Paper Mill
Location: Espanola, Spanish River, Sudbury County
When Built: 1905
Current Use: Milling operations
Access: Exterior views, tours available

GPS Location: N 46° 16.198' W 81° 46.576'
Directions: On Highway 6 going south into Espanola, you cross a bridge over the South River. Look to your left (East) and you will see the massive Domtar Paper Mill.

History: The mill was built in 1905 by the Spanish River Pulp and Paper Mill. It was purchased by the E.B. Eddy Co. in 1969 and became part of Domtar Inc. in 1998. The plant was extensively modernized in 1999.

Photography Tips: If you park in the pull off at the north end of the bridge, you can walk to the middle of the bridge and get a wide view of the mill and river. A lens in the range of about 28-70mm will be useful.

Nearby Attractions:
The Manitowaning Roller Mills are about an hours drive onto Manitoulin Island.

Self Guided Tours

Bruce County Tour (Half Day)
Number of Mill Sites - 9
Total Driving Time - 3 hours
Total Walking Time - Minimal

Bruce County contains a good number of interesting old mills, and a few of them are relatively unknown to those interested in them.

We start our tour at the Mildmay Chopping Mill in the village of Mildmay at GPS position N 44° 02.216' W 81° 07.015'.

Go north on Adam St off of County Rd 28. It is only a short distance down the lane.

This interesting old mill is presently unused but the owner is a timber worker who plans on renovating it. Our next stop is the Pinkerton Mill which is at GPS position N 44° 12.813' W 81° 16.144'.

From Mildmay, head northeast on Adam St toward Church St for 300 m. and take the 1st right onto Church St. and then turn left onto Elora St/ON-9 W. Continue to follow ON-9 W for 9.0 km and then turn left onto Bruce Road 4/Kincardine Hwy/ON-9 W Continue to follow Bruce Road 4/ON-9 W. for 4.1 km and then turn right onto County Road 3 (signs for Paisley/Southampton) where you continue for another 12.2 km and then left onto County Road 15 for 3.4 km. till you enter Pinkerton. The mill is beside the road on the Teeswater River.

The Pinkerton Mill is by the river. Next stop is the Fisher Grist Mill in Paisley. The GPS position is N 44° 18.382' W 81° 16.435'.

Head east on County Road 15 toward Bloor St for 3.4 km. and turn left onto County Road 3. Continue on for 10.9 km. and turn left onto Mill Dr/County Road 1. The mill is on the corner. You can also continue over the bridge and get a view from across the river.

Our next stop is Stark's Mill and it is only minutes away. The GPS position is N 44° 18.024' W 81° 16.782'.

Head southwest on Mill Dr/County Road 1 toward Victoria St S and continue to follow County Road 1 for 850 m. and you will see the mill on the left.

I think you will agree that Stark's Mill is one of the finest looking of Ontario's old mills with it's red coloured window frames setting it off beautifully. While our next stop, the Arranvale Mill, is not of the same quality, it is very interesting. It's GPS position is N 44° 27.276' W 81° 08.835'.

Head east on County Road 1 toward Wellington St and after 950 m. turn left onto Queen St S/County Road 3 and continue to follow County Road 3 for 15.2 km. Turn right onto County Road 17 (signs for Tara) and drive 13.5 km. and turn right onto Concession Road . Take the 1st right onto Mill Rd and after 950 m. you will see the mill on the left.

Our next stop is the McCullough Mill whose GPS position N 44° 32.113' W 81° 10.106'.

Head north on Mill Rd toward Concession Road 6 and then turn right onto Concession Road 6 and, after 450 m., take the 1st left onto County Road 10 and continue as it becomes Bruce Road 10 for 8.5 km. Turn left onto ON-21 S (signs for Ontario 21 S) and after 1.2 km., left on Thomas St. The mill is just over the bridge.

After this nicely weather textured mill, we will head for Parkhead Mill. The GPS position is N 44° 35.732' W 81° 09.829'.

Head east on ON-21 N toward Bruce Road 10 for 3.5 km. and turn left onto Grey Road 10 (signs for Bruce Road 10/Wiarton/Tobermory) and proceed for 6.2 km. Turn left onto Park Head Rd. and after 2.6 km. your destination will be on the right.

The Parkhead Mill is by the dam. Our next stop is McClure's Mill in Chesley. The GPS position is N 44° 17.886' W 81° 06.204'.

Head east on Park Head Rd toward Sideroad 5, and after 2.6 km. turn right onto County Road 10, which successively becomes Grey Road 10, Grey Bruce Line, County Road 40, and Grey Bruce Line again. After 28.6 km., turn right onto Concession Road 6. After another 2.1 km. turn left onto County Road 10, and then turn right onto 4 St NW after 4 km. and then left onto Thomas St. The mill is on the corner of Thomas St. and 2nd St. W.

Our last stop is the Scone Mill found at GPS position N 44° 18.317' W 81° 04.592'.

Head back northeast on Thomas St and turn right onto 4 St NW which becomes County Road 10. After 2.3 km., you will see the mill near the intersection with Mill Crescent in the village of Scone.

This mill was badly damaged in a flood in 2010.

This is the end of our tour.

Grey County Tour (Half Day)
Number of Mill Sites - 7
Total Driving Time - 2.5 hours
Total Walking Time - Minimal

This tour offers excellent variety of mills in the quiet of Grey County.

Our tour begins at the Ayton Mill in the Village of Ayton. It is located near off Arthur St, near the intersection of County Road 9/Mill St. The GPS position is N 44° 03.156'
W 80° 55.678'. Some of the best views are across the dam on the other side of the South Saugeen River. From here we will travel to the Neustandt Mill which is at GPS coordinates N 44° 04.521' W 81° 00.179'.

Head north on Arthur St/County Road 3 and proceed for 3.8 km and then turn left onto County Road 9 where you continue for 4.9 km. Continue onto Queen St for 500 m.and turn left onto Mill St/County Road 10 and continue for 300 m. The mill will be seen on your right.

The Neustandt Mill is over 150 years old but looks excellent in its bright coat of paint. Have a look at the antiques on the porch, and if they are open, inside the store. Our next stop is the Knechtel Feed Mill which is at GPS position N 44° 10.667' W 80° 49.008'.

Head northeast on Jacob St/County Road 10 toward Mill St and continue to follow County Road 10 for 300 m and then turn right onto Queen St (signs for Hanover) after 120 m. Take the 1st left onto David Winkler Pkwy/County Road 10 (signs for Hanover) and continue to follow County Road 10 for 8.9 km. Turn right onto 10th St/Grey Road 4/County Road 4 N and continue for 17.3 km. Continue as it becomes Durham Rd W for 450 m and then turn right onto Garafraxa St N/ON-6 S. After 600 m. turn left onto Mill St and take a quick left onto Albert St N. Albert St N turns right and becomes George St E and the mill will be seen on the right.

There is lots of space for unobstructed views around the mill and from the dam area behind. Our next stop will be Ferguson Gristmill and its GPS position is N 44° 13.749' W 80° 49.999'.

Head southwest on George St E toward Albert St N and then turn right onto Garafraxa St N/ON-6 N. Continue to follow ON-6 N for 6.9 km and you will reach a bridge over the Rocky Saugeen River. Find a safe place to pull off.

If you look to the southwest at the bridge, you will see the mill beside the bank. It is private property but their are good views from the bridge. What out for traffic. Our next stop is Welbeck Sawmill which is at GPS position N 44° 16.525' W 80° 53.540'.

Head north on ON-6 N and take the 1st left onto Sideroad 15 WGR. After 2.6 km. turn right onto Concession Road 2 WGR and after another 5.6 km turn left onto Welbeck Rd. The mill is less than a km. on the left.

The Welbeck Sawmill is a recent replacement for an older mill but it offers a lot to see. Our next stop is Williamsford Mill whose GPS position is N 44° 22.666' W 80° 52.285'.

Head east back the way you came on Welbeck Rd and travel 6.6 km to ON-6 N where you turn left. After 16.6 km. you reach the village of Williamsford and look for the mill on your left.

The Williamsford Mill houses a restaurant and bookstore. Our final destination is the Traverston Mill which is at GPS position N 44° 16.463' W 80° 44.514'.

Head south on ON-6 S toward Centre St for 13.0 km and turn left onto County Road 12. After 9.0 km turn right onto Traverston Rd and proceed 1.3 km. The mill is on the right.

This is the end of our Grey County Tour.

Cambridge Tour (Half Day)
Number of Mill Sites - 6
Total Driving Time - 25 minutes
Total Walking Time - 30 minutes

This tour offers some great places for lunch or a coffee during the middle walking portion. You could also bring a lunch and have it by the river.

Our trip begins at Sheave Tower and Blair Mill which is on Old Mill Rd in Blair between Blair Rd. and Meadow Creek Lane. Its GPS Position is N 43° 22.955' W 80° 23.364' After your visit to this fascinating site, drive as follows:

You can set your GPS as N 43° 21.779' W 80° 19.098' which will direct you as follows:

Head northeast on Old Mill Rd toward Ashton St (350 m) and make a slight right onto Blair Rd/Regional Road 42.

Continue to follow Regional Road 42 for 6.3 km and turn left onto Park Hill Rd W. Your destination will be on the left just over the bridge.

You can park in the lot at the corner of Blair Rd and Park Hill Rd. W.

The Dickson Mill is just over the bridge to the left (North). It has been recently renovated as a restaurant and you can see the old millrace as you walk across the bridge. When you reach the building, you can walk around and get an interesting and picturesque view from the back.

Our next stop is the Turnbull Mill Ruins, only a short distance away.

Cross Park Hill Rd. W. at the light, remaining on the river side of Water St. S. On the other side you will find the Turnbull Mill Ruins.

There are walkways through the ruins where you can explore the structure or relax for a few minutes by the river.

From here, we will head to the Galt Woolen Mill.

Continue south on Water St., passing Main St. which has a bridge over the Grand River, until you get to 36 Water St. South.

The Galt Woolen Mill now houses private offices. You can walk up the steps at the south end for a view of the back of the building and the Grand River. You will also have a fine view later in our tour from the other side of the river.

We now backtrack up Water St. to Main St. Turn left and cross the bridge. Turn left at the first intersection, Melville St. and proceed south to 7 Melville St.

This red brick building was once the site of the Riverside Silk Mill and now houses a School for Architecture. If you walk down the driveway at the south end, you will reach the river at the back. There is a wonderful view of the Galt Woolen Mill on the either side and you can see details of the old millrace.

Walk west for a block and you will come to Grand Ave. South. Go north for a few blocks and you will find yourself back at Park Hill Rd. where you parked your car. You will pass an open square which is bordered by beautiful old churches.

Once you have retrieved your car, we will drive to the American Standard Mill. You can set your GPS to N 43° 25.877' W 80° 18.648'

Head east on Park Hill Rd W toward Grand Ave N (350 m) and turn left onto Ainslie St N/ON-24 N/Regional Road 24. Continue to follow Regional Road 24 for 6.4 km and turn right onto Queen St W (signs for Queen Street) Destination will be on the left at the corner of Queen St W and Guelph Ave after another 2 km.

You should find parking on the street at this site. Take a walk along the path across the Speed River from the mill. There are some excellent views which include the dam.

This ends our tour.

Niagara Region Tour (Half Day)
Number of Mill Sites - 7
Total Driving Time - 1 hour
Total Walking Time - 15 minutes

This tour not only includes seven mill sites but three wonderful waterfalls, and you can easily add Niagara Falls as well. Our tour starts at Ball's Falls Conservation Area. You can set your GPS at N 43° 08.001' W 79° 22.946'

Take Exit 64 for Ontario Street toward County Road 18/Beamsville, and keep right at the fork and merge onto Ontario St. Turn right onto N Service Rd and after about 6 km., turn right onto Victoria Ave. After another 6 km. turn left onto 6 Ave/Regional Road 75. Balls Falls Conservation Area is a short distance and you will find parking in the lot.

There are two mill sites at Ball's Falls, one of which is a ruins. The Gristmill was built in 1809 and is just across the road from the parking lot. Don't forget to have a look at the spectacular Ball's Falls just nearby. The ruins of Ball's Falls Woolen Mill is across the road and upstream. You can skip it if you wish, but if you do go, you will be rewarded with the sight of a second wonderful waterfall, Ball's Falls Upper Waterfall. The trail is found across the road and on the other side of Twenty Mile Creek. A short pleasant walk will bring you to the ruins near the creek and the falls are just upstream from there.

Our next stop is Morningstar Mill. You can set your GPS at N 43°6.617 W 79° 15.816'.

Backtrack on Regional Road 75 till you reach Victoria Ave. and turn left. After about 2 km., make a left onto 8 Ave. After 5.2 km. continue onto Regional Road 69, and after 2.8 km., continue onto Pelham Rd. After 2.3 km., turn right onto First Louth St and another 1 km. continue onto Decew Rd. You will see Morningstar Mill on your left and there is a parking area in front of it.

There is another excellent waterfall behind the mill. The Welland Mill is our next stop. It is at GPS N43° 7.560' W 79° 12.180'.

Head east on Decew Rd toward Faywell Rd and after 1.7 km turn left onto Merrittville Hwy/Regional Road 50. After another 1.1 km, turn right onto St Davids Rd/Regional Road 71. 3.6 km and you will turn right onto Pine St N. The Welland Mill is at 20 Pine St. N. You will find parking beside the building or across the road

After having a look at the Welland Mill, you might want to wander around the buildings behind it as there are some interesting historical structures After that we are going to go to St Catharines to visit the Lybster Mill and the Old Merriton Cotton Mill which are conveniently across from each other and only a short distance away. You can set your GPS to N 43° 7.980' W 79° 11.964'.

Head north on Pine St N toward Ann St and after 400 m. take the 1st right onto St Davids Rd W/Regional Road 71. After another 350 m. turn left onto Ormond St N. Ormond St. becomes Merrit St at the intersection with Townline East, and this is our destination.

The Lybster Mill has been renovated as a Keg Restaurant and most of the exterior building including the smokestack has been retained. The Old Merriton Cotton Mill is across the street, also now a restaurant. Behind this building you may find traces of the Second Welland Canal which provided the water power for both mills.

Our final destination is the Secord Mill and its GPS position is N 43° 09.144' W 79° 06.256'

Continue north Merritt St and after 1.4 km., turn right onto Glendale Ave/Regional Road 89. Take the ramp onto the QEW and after 1.2 km, go left left onto ON-405 E (signs for Queenston Lewiston U.S.A). Go 5.0 km and take the Stanley Avenue/Regional Road 102 exit toward Niagara Falls/Niagara-on-the-Lake. After 500 m., turn left onto Stanley Ave/Regional Road 102 and then turn left onto Stamford Townline/Regional Road 100 (signs for ON-405/Toronto/County Road 61/Niagara Town Line), After 1.1 km
turn right onto Four Mile Creek Rd/Regional Road 100. The mill is at 137 Four Mile Creek Rd, St. Davids. There are no parking lots nearby, and you need to be careful of traffic.

Although it looks like a private dwelling, it was built as a mill in 1783, making it one of Ontario's oldest surviving mills. It was operated by Peter Secord, father of the Canadian heroine, Laura Secord. Many of the mills in the region were burned by the Americans but it escaped that fate.

This brings our tour to an end. Niagara Falls and Niagara on the Lake are nearby and offer much of interest.

Peterborough County Tour (Half Day)
Number of Mill Sites - 4
Total Driving Time - 2.5 hours
Total Walking Time - Minimal

Although this short tour only includes 4 mills, they are interesting and varied

Our tour begins at Needler's Mill. In the town of Millbrook turn south from King St.
(County Rd. 21) on Needler's Lane and the mill is a short distance at the end. The GPS position is N 44° 8.963' W 78° 26.868'. This is a charming building and in excellent shape. Our next stop is the Lang Mill which is at GPS position N 44° 16.572' W 78° 10.278'.

Head east on Needler's Ln toward Distillery St and turn left onto Distillery St and then turn right onto King St E/County Road 21 and continue for 8.7 km. Turn right onto 4 Line and travel 5.1 km. to County Road 2 where you turn left. Travel 13.2 km. and turn left onto Heritage Line/County Road 34. Another 3.5 km and you will turn right onto Lang Rd which proceed s to Lang Mill Conservation Area where the mill is located.

Our next stop from Lang Mill is close by. It is the Hope Sawmill and it is found at GPS position N 44° 17.280 ' W 78° 10.260'.

Turn back onto N Lang Rd and continue north for 1.1 km. Turn right onto Hope Mill Rd and after 650 m. take the 2nd left onto River Rd. The entrance to Hope Sawmill Conservation area is just a short distance.

This excellent sawmill with the dam beside it is an excellent place for lunch or a snack. Our last stop is Fowld's Mill which is at GPS position N 44° 18.631' W 77° 57.294'.

Head south on River Rd and turn left onto Hope Mill Rd. After 2.8 km. turn right onto Settlers Line and after another 2.9 km. turn left onto County Road 2. Continue 14.5 km. and then turn right onto Victoria St. After 210 m turn left onto Front St E where you will find the Fowld's Mill.

The mill has been renovated as a private residence but there are easy views from public area.

This is the end of our tour.

Mississippi River Tour (Half Day)
Number of Mill Sites - 7
Total Driving Time - 15 minutes
Total Walking Time - 1 hour

We are not sending you on a riverboat!! There is a Mississippi River in Lanark County and our tour of seven mills makes only two stops, one at Almonte and one at Carleton Place. You can start at either spot but we'll start at Carleton Place.

You can set your GPS to N 45° 08.458' W 76° 08.728'. In Carleton Place go south on Bridge St. from County Rd 7B/ Townline Rd and make a left on Mill St. Find a place to park, there is plenty of places available along this street.

Our first mill is Boulton Brown Mill which is located by the corner Beckwith St. and Mill St. You will see a historical plaque nearby. This building has been renovated as condominiums and you cannot trespass on the property but you can get some fine views from the street.

Our next stop is the McCarthur Mill and it is only a few steps away. Continue northeast on Mill St. to the intersection of Princess St. You will see the solid structure of the McArthur Mill just opposite. There are fine open views of the building and some of the remaining water control equipment.

Our last Carleton Place stop is Gillie's Mill and again, it is close by. From the intersection with Princess St, go left and continue on Princess. You cross one bridge and come to another shortly. Just across the second bridge you can see Gillie's Mill. There are excellent clear views from here.

This is the last of our Carleton Place stops. Go back to your car and we will head to Almonte, you can set your GPS to N 45° 13.648' W 76° 11.991'.

Head southwest on Mill St toward Beckwith St and take the 1st right onto Bridge St. and then turn right onto Town Line Rd E/County Road 7B (signs for Town Line Road) and follow it for 1.3 km. Continue onto Regional Road 29 for 9.9 km and then turn right onto Almonte St/County Road 49 (signs for Almonte Street/March Road). Continue to follow County Road 49 for 850m and then turn left onto Mary St. Park near the bottom of the street.

The massive building at the bottom of the street is the Rosamond Mill. It now houses condominiums but in its day it was one of the largest woolen mills in the world. Beside it you will find the Mississippi Valley Textile Museum. If it is open, it is worth a visit.

After this stop, go up Mary St. and turn right on Main and then left on Mill St. The five storey building on the corner is the Victoria Woolen Mill. Notice that the upper two stories are a different color of brick. That is because they were added to the original building. If you walk behind the building, you will find a viewing platform overlooking a waterfall. It is easy to see why some many mills are along this stretch of river when you see the force of the water which would be available to power them.

There is a river walk that takes us to our next stop. Look for it nearby the platform and start walking toward the train bridge. As you reach the area of the bridge, look across the river and you will see the Maple Leaf Mill. There are excellent views and opportunities for photographs all along this stretch.

Our last Mill is the Thoburn Mill. Continue along the river walk to Queen St. and turn right on Little Bridge Street. The mill is the long two storey brick building at 83 Little Bridge St. It also has been renovated as condominiums.

This ends our tour of the mills of the mighty Mississippi!

Leeds and Grenville County Tour (Half Day)
Number of Mill Sites - 4
Total Driving Time - 1.5 hours
Total Walking Time - 10 Minutes

Although this tour includes only four mills, it includes one of the most unusual, a windmill that became a lighthouse, and also what may be the finest historical mill left in Ontario.

We'll start with the latter. The Delta Mill is a beautiful structure and still operates as a mill on occasion. It is located in the Village of Delta on County Rd. 42. Its GPS position is N 44° 36.577' W 76° 07.345'. This mill is worth spending some time at, it is full of interesting detail and the mill pond offers great reflections.

From here we'll proceed to Brockville to visit the Island City Mill and the Shepherd's gristmill, only a short distance from each other. You can set your GPS position to N 44° 35.234' W 75° 41.283'.

Head southwest on County Road 42 W toward Main St for 24.1 km and continue onto County Road 29 for 15.1 km. Turn left onto Court House Square/County Road 29 and then take the 1st right onto Court House Ave/County Road 29 and then the 1st right onto King St W/County Road 2. There is parking along the street.

Near 189 King St. W., there is an entrance to an alleyway that brings you to the Island City Mill. The spacious courtyard allows you to see it from all sides. if we walk back to King St. and turn right, and then a quick left on John St, we will find the Shepherd Gristmill a short distance away at the intersection of John and Water St. This small brick mill now serves as a restaurant.

The last mill on our tour is the Windmill Lighthouse and it is at GPS position N 44° 43.254' W 75° 29.220'.

Continue east on King St W which becomes County Road 2. Afterb19.7 km. turn right on Windmill Rd. and you will find the site 300m on the right. There is parking across the road.

The Windmill Lighthouse is not only an interesting building but played a part in Canada's history. You can read about it on the historical plaques, or go to the top if it is open.

This is the end of our tour.

Frontenac County Tour (Full Day)
Number of Mill Sites - 7
Total Driving Time - 3.5 hours
Total Walking Time - Minimal

Some of the best looking surviving mills of Ontario found in Ontario built by United Empire Loyalists. We start our tour from the Babcock Mill whose GPS position is N: 44° 16.336' W: 76° 43.147'. It is currently used as part of a museum exhibit in the town of Odessa. From here we will proceed to Jackson's Mill which is located at GPS position N 44° 17.806' W 76° 33.598'.

Head northwest on Bridge St toward Emma St and turn right onto Main St. and after 650 m. turn left onto County Road 6 (signs for Wilton Road/ON-401). After 450 m. turn left onto the Mud Lake Road S ramp to ON-401 E/Kingston and merge onto ON-401 E. Go 12.1 km. and take exit 611 for County Road 38/Gardiners Road toward Kingston/Sharbot Lake and then turn right onto Gardiners Rd/County Road 38 (signs for Gardiners Road). Continue to follow County Road 38 for 550 m. and take the 1st right onto McIvor Rd (signs for McIvor Road) and then go left onto Jackson Mill Rd. You will see the mill near the end of the road, about 1.1 km.

Jackson's Mill is a private residence you can view from the road. Our next stop is the Kingston Woolen Mill which is at GPS position N 44° 17.559' W 76° 26.629'.

Head south on Jackson Mill Rd toward Paige Rd and after 1.1 km turn right onto McIvor Rd and then left onto County Road 38. Drive 550 m and turn left to merge onto ON-401 E toward Cornwall. Go 5.3 km and take exit 617 for Division Street toward County Road 10/Kingston/Westport and then after 750 m turn right onto Division St. In 900 m you will turn left onto John Counter Blvd and go 1.2 km before taking the 3rd right onto Montreal St. Drive 1.1 km and turn left onto Rideau St and then another 800 m and take the 1st left onto Cataraqui St. The huge mill is at the bottom of the street.

The huge Kingston Woolen Mill is now being used for many commercial purposes. You can view it from all sides. Our next stop is Lower Brewers Mill and its GPS position is N 44° 23.341' W 76° 19.465'.

Head east on Kingston Mills Rd toward Station Rd and after 2.1 km turn left onto ON-15 N and proceed for 13.0 km. Turn left onto Washburn Rd (signs for Washburn Road) and the mill site is about 250m.

Lower Brewers Mill is in an interesting setting. After visiting it, we will proceed to Chaffey's Lock Mill which is at GPS position N 44° 34.755' W 76° 19.249'.

Head south on Washburn Rd toward ON-15 S and after 220 m turn left onto ON-15 N and travel for 34.2 km. Turn left onto Chaffeys Lock Rd/County Road 9 (signs for Chaffeys Lock Road) and continue for 8.7 km. The mill is at the end of the road.

Chaffeys Lock is an interesting place to spend some time and ideal for a picnic lunch. Our next stop is one my favorite mills, the Bedford Mill. Its GPS position is N 44° 36.241' W 76° 24.346'.

Head east on County Road 9 toward Herman Rd and after 8.7 km turn left onto ON-15 N and go 2.6 km. Turn left onto County Road 42 W (signs for Newboro/Westport) and drive for 7.5 km then turn left onto Hutchings Rd and travel another 5.6 km. When you reach County Road 10 turn left and continue for 1.7 km. Turn right at signs for Bedford Mills and the site is 450 m down the road.

Bedford Mills is one of the best Ontario sites with its outbuildings and waterfall by a beautiful tree lined pond. Our last destination is the Bell Rock Mill whose GPS position is N 44° 28.562' W 76° 45.742'

Head south toward Perth Rd/Regional Road 10 and turn right and then go 22.0 km and turn right onto Rutledge Rd/Regional Road 5. Continue on follow Regional Road 5 for 15.4 km and then turn right onto County Road 38 and travel for another 8.3 km. Turn left onto Bellrock Rd/County Road 7 (signs for Bell Rock Road) and after 5.5 km make a slight right onto 1 Lake Rd. After 450 m take the 1st right onto Mill St and the mill is a short distance.

The Bell Rock Mill lacks the stately appearance of some of the mills we have seen, its textures and lines make up for it.

This is the end of our tour.

Hastings County Tour (Half Day)
Number of Mill Sites - 6
Total Driving Time - 3 hour
Total Walking Time - Minimal

Hastings County contains some of the finest mills in Ontario. We start our tour in Stockdale where the Cold Creek Lumber Mill and the Stockdale Mill are located. You can set your GPS to N 44°11.702' W 77°37.654'.

From Highway-401, take exit 522 for Wooler Road/County Road 40 and continue to follow County Road 40 until Miron Rd. where you turn right. After 1.2 km take the 1st left onto Broatch Crew Rd. and continue onto Parks Rd. After 1.6 km turn left onto Stockdale Rd and after another 4.3 km, you will find the mills on the left just past Maybee Rd.

The Stockdale Mill is on the right as you face upstream. It is in excellent shape and has been renovated as a cafe. On the opposite bank is the abandoned Cold Creek Lumber Mill.
Our next stop is the King's Mill at GPS position N 44°19.929' W 77°37.729'.

Continue onto Stockdale Rd for 500 m. turn right onto County Road 5. After 3.3 km., turn left onto River Dr/County Road 33 and continue for 11.2 km. Turn left onto W Front St/County Road 8 and take the 1st right onto Campbellford Rd/County Road 8 Continue to follow County Road 8 for 5.6 km and turn right onto Wellmans Rd/County Road 19. After 3.3 km, you will reach the intersection of King's Mill Rd and the mill will be on the right.

This is a fine looking building and a great place for a picnic. After you've had your fill, we'll proceed to O'Hara Mill at GPS position N 44°30.996' W 77°31.499'

Head north on Wellmans Rd/County Road 19 for 5.6 km and turn left onto Stirling Marmora Rd/County Road 14. Continue to follow Stirling Marmora Rd for 15 km and turn right onto Matthew St/Trans-Canada Hwy/ON-7 E. Follow Trans-Canada Hwy/ON-7 E for 11.5 km and turn left onto Jarvis Rd. After 1.4 km turn right onto Mill Rd. After about 1.7 km, you will see the entrance for O'Hara Mill. Go to the parking lot and take the short trail to the mill.

There are excellent spots to view and photograph this mill and its waterwheel. Our next stop is the Meyers Mill whose GPS position is N 44°10.270' W 77°22.960'.

Head east on Mill Rd toward Johnston Rd and after 3.1 km turn right onto ON-62 S. After another 2.6 km turn left onto St Lawrence St W/County Road 23/ON-62 S and then take the 1st right onto Durham St S/ON-62 S. Continue to follow ON-62 S for 40.2 km and turn left onto Station St (signs for ON-37/ON-2). After 260 m. the mill will be on the left.

This is a fine spot along the river. Our final destination is the Lonsdale Mill found at GPS position N 44°16.448' W 77°07.566'.

Head back northwest on Station Stand take the 1st right onto Pinnacle St/ON-62 N (signs for ON-401). Continue to follow ON-62 N and after 2.5 km merge onto ON-401 E via the ramp to Kingston. After 23 km take exit 566 for ON-49 toward Marysville Road/Deseronto/Picton and after 500 m. turn left onto ON-49 N (signs for Marysville Road) and continue for till Waddingham Rd where you make a left. Go 1.4 km and turn right onto Melrose Rd, which continues onto Marysville Rd, Shortly after Marysville Rd makes a sharp right, look for the mill on your right by the river.

While the Lonsdale Mill is on private property, there are excellent views from the road. This is the end of our tour.

Lake Simcoe Tour (Full Day)

Number of Mill Sites - 9
Total Driving Time - 4.5 hours
Total Walking Time - 10 minutes

There are a good number of historic mills that have survived in the Lake Simcoe area and we suggest you set aside a full day to see them.

Our tour starts at the Nicolston Gristmill which is located at 5140 5th Line, Alliston. The GPS position is 44° 10.093' W: 79° 48.701'. This mill site is especially rich in artifacts to be found around it. Our second stop is the Bell Gristmill whose GPS position is N 44° 19.695' W 79° 50.072'.

Head north on Line 5 toward Underhill Ct for 11.4 km. and turn left to stay on Line 5. After 4.2 km turn right onto Sideroad 25 and proceed for another 1.4 km where you take the 1st left onto 6 Line. After 2.6 km turn right onto Old Mill Rd and the entrance road to the mill is about 250 m.

The Bell Gristmill is a short walk, just over the dam. It is a very interesting structure. Recover your car and we are going to head for the Hillsdale Mill whose GPS position is N 44° 35.143' W 79° 44.121'.

Head west on Old Mill Rd toward 6 Line for 250 m and then turn right onto 6 Line and go 1.5 km to County Road 90 E and make a right. Go for 11.7 km and turn left to merge onto ON-400 N. After 6.7 km take the exit onto ON-400 N toward ON-69/Parry sound/Sudbury. Go 17.1 km and take exit 121 to merge onto Penetanguishene Rd/ON-93 N toward Midland/Penetanguishene. After 4.0 km turn right onto Mill St E and then continue onto Mt St Louis Rd W for 2.6 km. Turn right onto 2 Line N and after 600 m
you will reach the mill.

The Hillsdale Mill is exciting for photographers with it red painted exterior, weathered and dilapidated in parts. Our next stop is the Coldwater Mill which is at GPS position
N 44° 42.490' W 79° 38.614'.

Head northwest on 2 Line N toward Mt St Louis Rd W for 600 m and turn right onto Mt St Louis Rd W. After 7.2 km turn left onto the Ontario 400 ramp to Parry Sound N and travel 8.6 km on ON-400 N. Take exit 141 for Regional Road 23 toward ON-12 E/Coldwater/Fesserton/Vasey Road and after 700 m turn right onto Trans-Canada Hwy/County Road 23/ON-12 E which continues onto Sturgeon Bay Rd for 1.1 km. Turn right onto Coldwater Rd and then take the 1st right onto Mill St. The mill is a short distance.
The Coldwater Mill has been renovated as a restaurant and there are historical plaques which relate its history. Our next stop is Marchmont Mill and the GPS position is N 44° 37.966' W 79° 30.587'.

Head east on Mill St toward Coldwater Rd and turn right onto Coldwater Rd. After 1.2 km turn left onto Trans-Canada Hwy (signs for ON-400 E) and travel 13.6 km where you make a left onto Town Line and then take the 3rd right onto Marchmont Rd. The mill is less than a kilometer.

The Marchmont Mill hangs over the water and has been renovated as a private residence. The next stop is the Washago Gristmill and its GPS position is N 44° 45.001'
W 79° 19.812'.

Head southwest on Marchmont Rd toward Hume St for 800 m and turn left onto Town Line. Go another 600 m and turn left onto Trans-Canada Hwy/ON-12 S. After traveling 6.0 km take the Ontario 11 N ramp to Gravenhurst and merge onto ON-11 N and after 18.3 km. take the County Road 169 S exit toward Washago/ON-11 S. After 250 m. turn right onto County Road 169 and then take the 3rd left onto Grist Mill Rd. The mill is at the end of the road.

The Washago Gristmill is a private residence but you can view it from public areas. Our next stop is Udora Mill whose GPS position is N 44° 15.648' W 79° 10.650'.

Head southwest on Grist Mill Rd toward County Road 169 and turn left. After 24.4 km turn left onto Trans-Canada Hwy/ON-12 S and proceed for 23.2 km. Turn right onto ON-48 S (signs for Sutton/Toronto) and after 8.6 km turn left onto Durham Road 23/Lake Ridge Rd/Regional Road 23 (signs for Uxbridge). Continue to follow Lake Ridge Rd/Regional Road 23 for 8.6 km and then turn right onto Ravenshoe Rd/Regional Road 32 (signs for Ravenshoe Road)and go another 1.9 km where you take the 1st right onto Mill Pond Ln. The mill is about 400 m.

The Udora Mill is also known as the Peers Grist Mill. Our next stop is the Baldwin Mill which is found at GPS position N 44° 15.704' W 79° 20.671'.
Head west on Mill Pond Ln toward York St and after 400 m turn right onto Ravenshoe Rd/Regional Road 32 and continue for 13.2 km. Turn right onto ON-48 N and travel for 4.6 km. When you cross the Black River, the mill can be seen along the banks. Find a safe place to park.

The Baldwin Mill is a private residence but you have nice wide views from the road. Our last stop is the Sutton Mill whose GPS position is N 44° 18.294' W 79° 21.654'

Head north on ON-48 N toward Baldwin Rd and proceed 4.1 km. Turn left onto High St/Regional Road 9 (signs for High Street/Sutton) and the mill will be on the right after 1.1 km.

The Sutton Mill is our last stop on this tour.

Index

Aberfoyle Mill	72
Adam's Mill	181
Allan's Mill Ruins	73
Alton Mill	127
American Standard Mill	58
Ancaster Old Mill	98
Apps Mill	13
Armstrong Mill	74
Arranvale Mill	17
Arva Flourmills	75
Asselstine Woolen Mill	191
Austin Saw Mill	92
Ayton Mill	27
Babcock Mill	147
Backhouse Mill	52
Baechler Sawmill	59
Balaclava Mill	185
Baldwin Mill	199
Ball's Falls Gristmill	111
Ball's Falls Woolen Mill Ruins	112
Ball's Mill	121
Barber's Mill	93
Beach's Sawmill	192
Beatty Gristmill	35
Beatty Mill	76
Beaumont Knitting Mill	94
Bedford Mill	148
Bell Gristmill	200
Bell Rock Mill	148
Bellamy's Mill	193
Benmiller	45
Birge Mills	77
Blackridge Mill	60
Bluevale Mill	46
Boulton Brown Mill	156
Bowe's Mil	186
Brooklin Flourmill	88
Bruce's Gristmill	136
Brussels Mill	48
Caledonia Mill	42

Cannon Knitting Mill	99
Canton Mill	122
Cataract Mill Ruins	128
Chaffey's Lock Mill	150
Cheltenham Mill	129
Chisholm Mills	182
Code's Mill	157
Cold Creek Lumber Mill	103
Coldwater Mill	201
Collie Mill Ruins	158
Collingwood Gristmill	202
Collingwood Saw Mill	203
Cream of Barley Mill	89
Darnley Gristmill Ruins	100
Deagle Mill	128
Dean Sawmill	113
Delta Mill	170
Dickson Mill	61
Dods' Knitting Mill	130
Domtar Paper Mill	210
Doon Mill	64
E.W.B. Snider	62
Eden Mills	78
Eganville Gristmill Ruins	187
Elora Mill	79
Erb's Grist Mill	63
Ferguson Gristmill	28
Ferrie Mill Ruins	64
Fisher Grist Mill	18
Fishers Mill Ruins	101
Flesherton Mill	29
Folmar Windmill	47
Fowld's Mill	132
Fraser Mill	186
Galt Woolen Mill	65
German Woolen Mill Ruins	14
Gillies Mill	159
Gledhill Woolen Mill	45
Glen Coe Mill	151
Glen Tay Mill	181
Glenora Mill	183
Goldie Mill Ruins	80

Gooderham and Worts Distillery	137
Gore Mills	101
Grove's Mill	83
Hammond Sawmill	86
Harrington Gristmill	66
Harris Woolen Mill Ruins	87
Herb Miller Saw Mill	30
Hillsdale Mill	204
Hilton Falls Mill Ruins	95
Holstein Mill	31
Hoopers Mill	177
Hope Sawmill	133
Hortop Mill	82
Inglis Falls Grist Mill Ruins	32
Island City Mill	171
Jackson's Mill	151
King's Mill	104
Kingston Woolen Mill	152
Knechtel Feed Mill	33
Lang Mill	134
Latta Mill Ruins	105
Lindsay Mill Ruins	110
Logan's Mill	48
Lonsdale Mill	106
Lower Brewers Mill	152
Lybster Mill	114
Maberly Sawmill	160
Maitland Mill	49
Manitowaning Roller Mills	197
Maple Leaf Mill	161
Marchmont Mill	205
Markham Cider Mill	138
Markham Saw Mill	139
Martintown Mill	194
McArthur Mill	162
McClure's Mill	20
McCullough Mill	19
McDougall Mill	188
Merrickville Ruins	163
Merritton Cotton Mill	115
Meyer's Mill	107
Mildmay Chopping Mill	21

Mill of Kintail	164
Molson Mill	123
Morningstar Mill	116
Needler's Mill	135
Neustadt Mill	34
Newburgh Mill	177
Nicolston Gristmill	206
O'Hara Mill	108
Old Killaloe Mill	189
Old Mill at Toronto	140
Old Stone Mill	170
Orchardville Mill	35
Otterville Mill	53
Paisley City Roller Mills	25
Parkhead Chopping Mill	22
Peers Grist Mill	208
Petworth Mill Ruins	154
Pfrimmer Mill	45
Pinkerton Mill	23
Plattsville Grist Mill	54
Port Perry Grain Elevator	126
Pratt's Mill	124
Priest's Mill	195
Purdy Mill	125
Quance Mill	43
Riverside Silk Mill	67
Roblin's Mill	141
Roddick Mill Ruins	172
Rosamond Mill	165
Rosamond Mill 1	167
Schomberg Feed Mill	142
Scone Mill	24
Scott's Mill	184
Secord Mill	118
Sheave Tower/Blair Mill	68
Shepherd's Gristmill	173
Snider's Cider Mill	143
South River Grist Mill	198
Spencerville Mill	174
St. Andrew's Mill	83
St. George Mill	15
St. Jacobs Mill	62

Stark's Mill	25
Stiver Mill	144
Stockdale Gristmill	109
Sutton Mill	207
Tay View Mill	186
Thamesford Mill	55
The Long Island Mill	180
Thoburn Mill	166
Thompson Paper Mill Ruins	177
Thornbury Mill	36
Tillson Pea Mill	56
Todmorden Mills	145
Traverston Mill	37
Turnbull Ruins	69
Tyrone Mill	90
Udora Mill	208
Union Flour Mills Ruins	178
Van Alstine Mill	183
Vanstone Mill	91
Varna Mill	51
Walters Falls Mill	38
Washago Grist Mill	209
Washburn Mill	153
Watson's Mill	180
Welbeck Sawmill	39
Welland Mill	119
Wellesley Feed Mill	70
Williams Mill	96
Williamsford Mill	40
Windmill Lighthouse	175
Wissler's Mill	84
Wood's Mill	169

www.ingramcontent.com/pod-product-compliance
Lightning Source LLC
Chambersburg PA
CBHW062200080426
42734CB00010B/1761